PERSPECTIVES

PRE-INTERMEDIATE

Workbook

NATIONAL
GEOGRAPHIC
LEARNING

Australia · Brazil · Canada · Mexico · Singapore · United Kingdom · United States

NATIONAL GEOGRAPHIC LEARNING

Perspectives Pre-Intermediate

Publisher: Sherrise Roehr

Executive Editor: Sarah Kenney

Project Managers: Katherine Carroll,
Ruth Goodman

Development Editor: Kerry Maxwell

Media Researcher: Leila Hishmeh

Senior Technology Product Manager:
Lauren Krolick

Director of Global Marketing: Ian Martin

Senior Product Marketing Manager:
Caitlin Thomas

Sr. Director, ELT & World Languages:
Michael Burggren

Production Manager: Daisy Sosa

Senior Print Buyer: Mary Beth Hennebury

Composition: Lumina Datamatics, Inc.

Cover/Text Design: Brenda Carmichael

Art Director: Brenda Carmichael

Cover Image: Bernardo Galmarini/
Alamy Stock Photo

© 2018 National Geographic Learning, a part of Cengage Learning

ALL RIGHTS RESERVED. No part of this work covered by the copyright herein may be reproduced or distributed in any form or by any means, except as permitted by U.S. copyright law, without the prior written permission of the copyright owner.

"National Geographic", "National Geographic Society" and the Yellow Border Design are registered trademarks of the National Geographic Society
® Marcas Registradas

For product information and technology assistance, contact us at
Cengage Learning Customer & Sales Support, cengage.com/contact

For permission to use material from this text or product,
submit all requests online at **cengage.com/permissions**
Further permissions questions can be emailed to
permissionrequest@cengage.com

Pre-Intermediate Workbook

ISBN: 978-1-337-28898-9

National Geographic Learning
Cheriton House, North Way,
Andover, Hampshire, SP10 5BE
United Kingdom

National Geographic Learning, a Cengage Learning Company, has a mission to bring the world to the classroom and the classroom to life. With our English language programs, students learn about their world by experiencing it. Through our partnerships with National Geographic and TED Talks, they develop the language and skills they need to be successful global citizens and leaders.

Locate your local office at **international.cengage.com/region**

Visit National Geographic Learning online at **NGL.Cengage.com/ELT**
Visit our corporate website at **www.cengage.com**

Printed in the United Kingdom by CPI Antony Rowe
Print Number: 01   Print Year: 2023

1A He's really into music

VOCABULARY Personality

1 Revision Choose the best words to complete the sentences.

1 My father has no hair. He's *bald / beard / brown*.
2 My sister is *long / tall / curly*. She can touch the ceiling in her bedroom.
3 **A** Does your brother have *bald / a beard / glasses*?
   B No, he doesn't like hair on his face.
4 My hair isn't straight. It's *short / blonde / curly*.
5 My mother, brother and I all have dark hair, but my father's hair is different. It's *black / blonde / long*.
6 I wear *a beard / glasses / short hair*, but only when I'm reading.

2 Revision Look at the photos. Match the descriptions with the people.

a

b

c

d

e

f

1 Carlos has long, curly brown hair and a beard. _____
2 Angela is tall and has long, curly blonde hair. _____
3 Richard has very short dark hair. _____
4 Lily has short, straight, dark hair. _____
5 Nick is tall and bald, and he has a beard. _____
6 Emma has long, straight, brown hair and glasses. _____

3 Complete the adjectives to describe personality.

1 fr __ __ n __ __ __ __
2 s __ c __ ab __ __
3 con __ __ __ en __
4 t __ __ en __ __ d
5 e __ s __ -g __ __ __ __ g
6 n __ __ v __ __ s
7 p __ __ u __ __ r
8 in __ __ __ __ __ g __ __ t
9 ch __ __ __ f __ __
10 r __ __ __ x __ __

4 Write the word that means the opposite of each description. There is one word you don't need.

intelligent	lazy	loud	nasty
nervous	serious	shy	weak

1 kind, helpful _____
2 active, hard-working _____
3 funny, cheerful _____
4 sociable, confident _____
5 calm, relaxed _____
6 quiet _____
7 strong _____

5 Look at the sentences and photos in Exercise 2. Choose the best word to describe each person.

1 Lily is *active / lazy*.
2 Emma is *intelligent / loud*.
3 Angela is *kind / nervous*.
4 Carlos is *serious / funny*.
5 Richard is *calm / hard-working*.
6 Nick is *cheerful / nasty*.

6 Read the sentences. Are the adjectives logical (L) or not logical (N)?

1 I don't understand the maths lesson and I don't have time to study. I'm very <u>confident</u> about the test tomorrow! _____

2 A <u>nasty</u> friend is usually fun to be with. _____

3 Good teachers are <u>kind</u> to their students. _____

4 A good worker is <u>lazy</u>. _____

5 It's always good to be <u>honest</u> when you answer a question. _____

6 A popular person is usually very <u>sociable</u>. _____

7 A <u>shy</u> person feels nervous talking to new people.

_____

8 It's not easy for an <u>intelligent</u> person to understand new ideas. _____

7 Listen to the descriptions. Complete the sentence with the correct form of *be* and the adjective that best fits each description. There are two adjectives you don't need. 🎧 **1**

| active | easy-going | funny | helpful | honest |
| lazy | loud | | nasty | shy | talented |

1 Our teacher _____.

2 We _____.

3 The neighbours _____.

4 My flatmate _____.

5 My aunt _____.

6 You _____.

7 My boss _____.

8 I _____.

8 **Extension** Put the adjectives into the correct category.

affectionate	annoying	careless	generous
impatient	organized	patient	polite
rude	selfish		

Positive personality traits	Negative personality traits

9 **Extension** Listen to the descriptions. Circle all the adjectives that describe each person. 🎧 **2**

1 Homer   intelligent / lazy / careless / organized / helpful / selfish / generous

2 Marge   kind / helpful / active / affectionate / annoying / patient / selfish

3 Bart   generous / rude / clever / funny / honest / annoying / hard-working

4 Lisa   talented / intelligent / nasty / hard-working / polite / impatient / neat

PRONUNCIATION -*s* verb endings

10 Listen and choose the verb that has the same ending sound. 🎧 **3**

1 **a** goes
b thinks
c dances

2 **a** follows
b acts
c fixes

3 **a** enjoys
b sits
c touches

4 **a** plays
b looks
c watches

5 **a** feels
b jumps
c misses

6 **a** sees
b puts
c practises

7 **a** calls
b stops
c changes

8 **a** wears
b laughs
c wishes

LISTENING

11 Listen and choose the correct words to complete the sentence. 🎧 **4**

1 He's _____.
  a honest
  b friendly
  c hard-working

2 She's into _____.
  a music
  b art
  c sport

3 He's a bit _____.
  a intelligent
  b loud
  c shy

4 He's into _____.
  a sport
  b books
  c photography

5 She's very _____.
  a popular
  b fit
  c kind

6 She enjoys _____.
  a writing
  b walking
  c drawing

7 He's _____.
  a cool
  b serious
  c nervous

8 She really likes _____.
  a dancing
  b singing
  c reading

12 Listen and complete each sentence with the name(s) and the correct verb in the present tense. 🎧 **5**

| be | like (x2) | paint |
| think | want (x2) | |

1 _____ to go to the cinema.

2 _____ busy this afternoon.

3 _____ fruit and flowers.

4 _____ painting is difficult.

5 _____ action movies.

6 _____ DJ Spooky.

7 _____ to meet up tomorrow.

13 Listen. Are the sentences true (T) or false (F)? 🎧 **6**

1 The passage explains why we don't like some things. _____

2 People like something only because it looks, smells, sounds or tastes good. _____

3 What people think about something makes them like or dislike something. _____

4 People often believe that expensive things are good. _____

5 People like things that they connect with positive experiences. _____

14 Correct the false sentences in Exercise 13. Listen again if necessary. 🎧 **6**

15 Listen to the lecture and choose the correct options. 🎧 **7**

1 What is the lecture mainly about?
  a the United States of America in the 1930s
  b different characters from California
  c characters and personalities in a book
  d being a leader of a family

2 Why does the professor say this: 'novel or long story'?
  a The students had two tasks.
  b The novel is not true.
  c The book has many stories.
  d A novel is a long story.

3 Why did farmers leave their homes?
  a There was not enough rain.
  b Land was cheap in California.
  c They were angry with their neighbours.
  d A fire burned their crops and fields.

4 What does the professor probably think when he says this:
'It's not easy to leave your home.'?
  a People move around a lot.
  b Most of the professor's students live abroad.
  c Most people enjoy staying in the place they know.
  d Some people enjoy the weather at home.

5 What does the professor mean when he says this:
'move their whole family across the country'?
  a The farmers had to move to a new country.
  b The farmers had to leave the United States of America.
  c The farmers had to move to a new place in the United States of America.
  d The farmers had to find a state with more rain.

6 There are two answers for the next question.
Mark two answers.
Which personality words does the professor say in the lecture?
  a fearful   **d** helpful
  b calm   **e** shy
  c brave   **f** honest

GRAMMAR Present simple and present continuous

16 Read the sentences and decide if the action is taking place right now (RN) or is a general truth (GT).

1 Julia is working on an article for her school's website. _____
2 She is writing about the new students in her class this term. _____
3 Julia's school welcomes new students at the beginning of each term. _____
4 There are three new students in Julia's class this term. _____
5 Alex is funny, laughs a lot and tells jokes when he meets new people. _____
6 Min smiles a lot and seems really happy to be in the class. _____

17 Complete the sentences with the present simple form of these verbs.

be	create	go	hope
mind	practise	study	think
want			

1 Naomi _____ to the best school in the city.
2 She _____ a lot because she wants to go to university.
3 She _____ to study computer science.
4 Sometimes she _____ the only girl in her class.
5 But she _____ not _____ because she _____ computers are really interesting.
6 She _____ that she can show other girls that computer science is cool.
7 Naomi _____ coding at home.
8 She _____ new apps for her friends to try.

18 Choose the correct verb forms for each sentence.

1 Bo has a new camera and _____ how to take better photos. He _____ to take photos of people.
   a is learn; liking   c are learning; is like
   b is learning; likes   d learning; like
2 His friends Mina and Jacob _____ him. They _____ to have their photo taken.
   a help; liking   c help; are liking
   b is helping; is liking   d are helping; like

3 Right now, Mina and Jacob _____ in front of a statue. They _____ taking selfies.
   a standing; enjoying   c stand; enjoying
   b are standing; enjoy   d stands; enjoys
4 For some reason, Mina and Jacob _____, and Bo _____ annoyed.
   a not smiling; be   c are not smiling; is
   b is not smiling; is being   d doesn't smile; being
5 Now he _____ them to smile because they _____ happy.
   a ask; not looking   c is ask; look
   b is asking; do not look   d is asking; no looking
6 They _____ to the park now because Bo _____ to take photos in front of the fountain.
   a walks; want   c are walking; wants
   b is walking; is wanting   d walking; wanting

19 Complete the sentences with the correct form of the verbs in brackets.

1 My brother really _____ (like) music and _____ (listen) to it all the time.
2 He _____ (play) the electric guitar and the drums. He's really talented!
3 He and his friends _____ (be) in a band and _____ (write) cool new songs.
4 My friend Mei plays keyboard and _____ (sing) in a band with my brother and his friend Maia. The name of their band _____ (be) Victory.
5 This month, they _____ (practise) all day every Saturday for their concert.
6 I _____ (not, can) watch them every time they practise because I _____ (study) for an important exam.
7 But I _____ (want) to go to their big concert on the 25th!
8 I _____ (not, know) how to play any instrument at the moment, but I _____ (learn) the keyboard. If I'm good, maybe I can join my brother's band!

20 Choose the correct words to complete the questions.

1 *Is / Does* he intelligent?
2 *Is / Are* your classmates kind?
3 *Do / Does* you like cool music?
4 *Does / Do* Simon play the guitar?
5 *Am / Is* I late for class?
6 *Does / Is* it raining?
7 *Do / Does* the DJs play good music?
8 *Are / Do* you a good singer?

1B How are you feeling?

VOCABULARY BUILDING Adjective complements

1 Put the words in the correct order to make sentences and questions.

1 you / angry / Are / results / your / about

_____

_____ ?

2 the / She's / about / test / worried

_____

_____ .

3 get / easily / children / Do / frightened

_____

_____ ?

4 They're / about / presentation / nervous / the

_____

_____ .

5 excited / holiday / about / We're / our

_____

_____ .

6 by / students / The / the / seemed / lecture / bored

_____

_____ .

7 news / I / when / on TV / watch / upset / I / become / the

_____

_____

_____ .

8 looks / about / He / angry / something

_____

_____ .

9 Karen / Is / of / dogs / afraid / big

_____

_____ ?

READING

2 Read the text and choose the correct options.

1 Why do Finnish researchers recommend that people spend about five hours a month outdoors?
   a in order to learn more about urban areas
   b so that they can stay healthy
   c because winters in Finland are very cold
   d because they work for the government

2 According to paragraph 4, which of the following is <u>not</u> true of the Saneum Healing Forest?
   a Visitors are offered a tea made from elm bark.
   b Visitors hike along creeks and through the forest.
   c Firefighters fought a fire there for three days.
   d Firefighters practise yoga in order to relax.

3 Which of the following best restates the saying 'Body and soil are one' in paragraph 4?
   a Being aware of our natural surroundings can help us remain healthy.
   b It's important to wash your hands at least once every day.
   c People who are careful about what they eat sometimes grow their own food.
   d Being clean is the most important thing you can do in order to stay healthy.

4 What did a study in Japan show about the effects of being outdoors?
   a A walk in the woods takes at least fifteen minutes.
   b Spending time outdoors can cause measurable changes in the body.
   c Forests and natural places are usually far from city centres.
   d People who live in city centres have high blood pressure.

3 Write the name of each country next to the correct statement.

Canada	Finland	Japan	South Korea

1 Researchers measured changes in the body caused by spending time outdoors.

_____

2 The government wants to know more about its people's moods.

_____

3 Researchers have found evidence that being outdoors contributes to the 'happiness effect.'

_____

4 Local governments pay for healthy outdoor experiences for their people.

_____

4 Match the information (a–e) with the paragraphs (1–5).

a measurable effects of being outdoors _____
b a question we all want answered _____
c the 'happiness effect' _____
d a weekly dose of nature _____
e a 'Healing Forest' _____

This is your brain on nature

1 🎧 8   What makes you happy? It's a question we all want an answer to. Does food make you happy? Do pictures of puppies make you feel calm? What about being outdoors, walking in the sun or hiking in a forest?

2 'People underestimate the happiness effect' of being outdoors, says Lisa Nisbet, a psychology professor at Canada's Trent University. 'We don't think of it as a way to increase happiness. We think other things will do this, like shopping or TV.' But there's a lot of evidence* to show that being outdoors in nature makes people feel better. In fact, some countries are promoting nature experiences as one way to help people stay healthy.

3 In Finland, a large number of people become sad or depressed in winter. The Finnish government wants to know why. It pays researchers to ask people about their moods after visiting natural and urban areas. Do they feel more nervous or more relaxed? The researchers studied people's responses. They are recommending a minimum nature dose* of five hours a month, or several short visits a week, to a natural place.

4 In South Korea, many people deal with stress from work and school. But this very hard-working nation respects nature. A very old saying reminds South Koreans that 'Shin to bul ee – Body and soil are one.' At the Saneum Healing Forest, east of Seoul, 'health rangers' offer visitors elm-bark tea, then take them on hikes along creeks and through forests of red maple, oak and pine-nut trees. During one visit, 40 firefighters take part in a free, three-day programme sponsored by the local government. After a morning of hiking, they enjoy practising yoga and arranging delicate dried flowers. Among them is Kang Byoung-wook, a 46-year-old firefighter from Seoul. 'It's a stressed life,' he says. 'I want to live here for a month.'

5 Researchers can measure how a fifteen-minute walk in the woods causes changes in the body. A study in Japan compares people who spend time in forests and in city centres. The people who spend time in nature show a lower level of stress, and lower blood pressure and heart rate. Yoshifumi Miyazaki, one of the researchers, believes our bodies relax in pleasant, natural surroundings because they are originally from natural places. When we slow down, stop working and take in beautiful natural surroundings, we often feel more cheerful and our mental* performance improves. Our senses are better at interpreting information about plants and streams, Miyazaki says, than traffic and high-rises!

evidence *a sign that shows something is true or correct*
dose *an amount of something, usually medicine*

mental *related to the mind*

1C I expect my friends to understand

GRAMMAR Verb patterns: verb + -*ing* or infinitive with *to*

1 Listen and complete the sentences. 🎧 9

1 When the musicians begin _____, you must stop talking.

2 Do you plan _____ after you graduate?

3 I always enjoy _____ to my friends after school.

4 He prefers _____ before dinner.

5 Oscar can't help _____ when he hears sad music.

6 Mei tries _____ her grandfather every week.

7 I hope _____ ten countries before my 21st birthday.

8 Young children learn _____ by listening to other people.

2 Choose the correct words to complete the sentences.

1 She usually manages *studying* / *to study* during the week so that she can relax at weekends.

2 I don't want *arguing* / *to argue* with you.

3 She enjoys *helping* / *to help* her younger sister.

4 He enjoys *going* / *to go* for a long run at the weekend.

5 Taavi wants *writing* / *to write* an email to his friend in Canada.

6 Can you learn *speaking* / *to speak* English on your own?

7 I don't mind *seeing* / *to see* that film again with you.

8 Lana avoids *going* / *to go* to the gym at weekends. It's so busy!

3 Complete the sentences with the verb + -*ing* or the infinitive with *to* form of the verbs in brackets.

1 My dad plans _____ (read) five books while he's on holiday.

2 Does he enjoy _____ (study) history?

3 I think it's possible to avoid _____ (tell) her about the surprise party.

4 Frank wants to start _____ (exercise) more, starting on 1st January.

5 Ted can't help _____ (laugh) every time Seth tells a joke.

6 Cara doesn't want _____ (share) a room with her younger sister.

7 Do you think you can manage _____ (get) your work done before Friday?

8 I promise _____ (come) to your party early. Then I can help you get ready.

9 Devan is beginning _____ (look) for a job.

4 Are the verbs in bold correct? Correct the incorrect verbs.

1 He enjoys **to go** on holiday with his family.
_____

2 I want **to see** that new film next weekend.
_____

3 Do you enjoy **trying** new restaurants?
_____

4 She needs to learn **eating** with chopsticks.
_____

5 Jim hates **going** to the cinema alone.
_____

6 I need **talking** to you about our homework for tomorrow.
_____

7 Does she want **to call** him or **to speak** to him in person?
_____

8 I'm trying to avoid **to spend** too much money on holiday.
_____

5 Put the words in the correct order to make sentences and questions.

1 hates / class / Jean / being / late / for
_____.

2 job / He / have / before / he / hopes / a / graduates / to
_____.

3 the / at / I / stop / need / shop / to
_____.

4 us / with / come / he / Does / to / want
_____?

5 loves / She / history / about / reading
_____.

6 checking / after / dinner / avoids / Emily / email / her
_____.

7 salad / He / a / eating / prefers / lunch / for
_____.

8 enjoy / you / subjects / difficult / Do / studying
_____?

6 Complete the conversations with the verb + -ing or the infinitive with *to* form of the verbs in brackets. Some sentences have two correct answers.

1 A What can I do when I feel sad?
  B I suggest _____ (go) for a long walk.

2 A Are you going to the beach this weekend? I really want to go!
  B I don't know. I promise _____ (call) you if I go.

3 A How's your homework going?
  B Well, I hate _____ (ask) for help, but it's really hard.

4 A Why don't you cycle to work?
  B I want to, but I need _____ (buy) a bike first!

5 A Do you read books by the author Isabelle Youngman?
  B I do. I often begin _____ (laugh) when I'm reading because her books are so funny.

6 A Do you want to get some sushi with me?
  B Yes! I love _____ (eat) sushi!

7 Read the questions. Choose the correct answer.

1 What are you doing?
  a I'm starting to make dinner.
  b I'm starting make dinner.

2 What are you doing this weekend?
  a I hope to see a film with my sister.
  b I hope seeing a film with my sister.

3 Do you want to study together for the test?
  a Sure! I don't mind to study with other people.
  b Sure! I don't mind studying with other people.

4 Do you have enough money to pay for the trip?
  a I think I can manage to save enough by next year.
  b I think I can manage saving enough by next year.

5 What should we do for dinner?
  a I want to go to the new Thai restaurant in town.
  b I want going to the new Thai restaurant in town.

6 Can you play the piano?
  a A little. I'm learning to play now.
  b A little. I'm learning playing now.

7 Do you want cake for dessert?
  a It looks so good! I'd like to trying a piece.
  b It looks so good! I'd like to try a piece.

8 Can you come to the party?
  a Yes, and I promise bringing some food.
  b Yes, and I promise to bring some food.

8 Choose the correct words to complete the sentences. In some sentences both answers are correct. Are any of the sentences true for you?

1 My friends and I like *helping / to help* each other.
2 I want *visiting / to visit* my grandparents in Poland this summer.
3 My parents want me *spending / to spend* more time studying.
4 They're right. I need *studying / to study* more.
5 It's easy *wasting / to waste* time on social media.
6 I avoid *using / to use* social media.
7 I don't enjoy *watching / to watch* films on my laptop.
8 I prefer *watching / to watch* them on TV or at the cinema.
9 In fact, the best place *watching / to watch* films is the new multi-screen cinema in my city.
10 I usually have a chance *going / to go* there every month.

9 Complete the sentences with a verb + -ing or an infinitive with *to* so they are true for you.

1 My family needs _____.
2 I need _____.
3 I want _____.
4 My friend wants _____.
5 I like _____.
6 I don't like _____.
7 I enjoy _____.
8 My friends and I enjoy _____.

1D Half a million secrets

TEDTALKS

AUTHENTIC LISTENING SKILLS

1 Listen to the TED Talk. Complete the sentences with these numbers. There are two that you don't need. 🎧 10

2004	3,000	half-million	2014
two	three	four	2,000

1 It all started with a crazy idea in November of
_____.

2 I printed up _____ self-addressed postcards.

3 You can see my wife struggling to stack a brick of postcards on a pyramid of over a _____ secrets.

4 I had this postcard posted on the PostSecret blog _____ years ago on Valentine's Day.

5 For _____ years, my girlfriend and I, we've made it this Sunday morning ritual to visit the PostSecret blog together…

6 My son's birth is on this camera. He turns _____ tomorrow.

WATCH ▶

2 Watch the TED Talk. Choose the correct words to complete the sentences.

1 People *make / are making* their own postcards.

2 Frank *shares / is sharing* people's secrets on PostSecret.

3 Frank *collects / is collecting* secrets on PostSecret right now.

4 People *send / are sending* him emails with secrets.

5 Matty *takes / is taking* the pictures off the cameras.

6 The man says his hands *shake / are shaking*.

3 Match the adjectives from the talk with the situations.

1	crazy	**a**	people who lose their cameras and pictures
2	special		
3	exuberant	**b**	Matty's idea
4	ingenious	**c**	Frank's idea in November of 2004
5	desperate	**d**	email of a family that Matty shows Frank
6	emotional		
		e	man asks girlfriend to marry him
		f	the secrets in Frank's collection

4 Are the sentences true (T) or false (F)?

1 People buy postcards from Frank. _____

2 PostSecret is hard to use. _____

3 Only people with special secrets can use PostSecret. _____

4 People can send lost cameras to Matty. _____

5 The pictures go back to the people who lost their cameras. _____

6 Matty and Frank work together. _____

5 Choose the correct answers.

1 What is the speaker mainly discussing?
 a how many people visit his blog a day
 b the secrets from his collection
 c why secrets are important

2 What is PostSecret?
 a a website
 b a place where people post their secrets
 c a place in Washington, DC

3 Why does the speaker mention Matty?
 a to talk about how students use PostSecret
 b to show that people in Canada use PostSecret
 c to explain how people's lives have changed through PostSecret

4 What is the speaker's opinion of IFoundYourCamera?
 a He doesn't think it is helpful.
 b He thinks it is important.
 c He thinks only people who like photos will use it.

5 What can be inferred about the speaker and PostSecret?
 a The speaker will continue to work on PostSecret.
 b The speaker will stop doing PostSecret to start another idea.
 c The speaker will sell the secrets on PostSecret.

6 Why does the speaker say this:
'Secrets can take many forms. They can be shocking or silly or soulful.'?
 a to explain that everyone has secrets
 b to explain a good secret
 c to explain that secrets are different

VOCABULARY IN CONTEXT

6 Match the words with the definitions.

1	struggling	**a**	a picture
2	calm	**b**	relaxed
3	proposal	**c**	when a person asks another person to marry him or her
4	image		
5	language barriers	**d**	the difficulties people have because they don't speak the same language
		e	to have a hard time with something

1E What are you into?

SPEAKING

Useful language

Talking about likes and dislikes

Are you into…	sports / music / gaming / cycling?
I play… I love to watch… I'm not that interested in… I don't mind… I can't stand…	tennis / basketball / football.
Do you have a favourite…	team / kind of music / place to go walking?
I'm really into…	Real Madrid / hip-hop / going to the mountains.
That's cool. / Really? / Wow!	

1 Put the words in the correct order to make sentences and questions.

1 into / Are / music / you

_____?

2 interested / I'm / in / not / gaming / that

_____.

3 basketball / to / I / watch / love

_____.

4 Do / a favourite / have / team / you

_____?

5 really / skating / into / I'm

_____.

6 cool / Wow, / that's

_____!

7 mind / don't / hip-hop / I

_____.

8 pop / I / stand / music / can't

_____.

2 Complete the sentences. Then listen and check your answers. 🎧 11

Are you into (x3)	Do you have a favourite (x2)
I can't stand	I don't mind
I love to (x3)	I'm not that interested in
I'm really into (x3)	I play

1 A _____ sports?
B _____ watch football.
_____ Real Madrid.

2 A _____ kind of music?
B _____ the saxophone
so _____ listen to jazz
music.

3 A _____ gaming?
B A bit. _____ playing games,
but _____ pro-gaming!
Watching other people play is so boring.

4 A _____ place to relax?
B _____ films so
_____ go to the cinema.

5 A _____ cycling?
B _____ road cycling, but
_____ mountain biking.

3 You are on holiday in another country and meeting new people.

Look at the questions from the conversations in Exercise 2. For each question, use the Useful language and make some notes about how you would answer it.

4 Write responses that are true for you. Use the Useful language.

1 Are you into sports?

_____
_____

2 Are you into clothes?

_____
_____

3 What are you into?

_____
_____

4 What kind of music do you like?

_____
_____

5 What kind of films do you like?

_____
_____

6 What TV programmes are you into?

_____
_____

5 Listen and follow the instructions. 🎧 12

Now listen to a model answer and compare it with your ideas. 🎧 13

WRITING An introductory postcard

6 Match the two parts of the sentences.

1	My name is	**a**	science and maths.
2	I'm from	**b**	about you?
3	I'm in year 9	**c**	Osaka City in Japan.
4	My favourite subjects are	**d**	favourite type of music?
5	I love watching	**e**	at secondary school.
6	I'm also	**f**	really into hip-hop.
7	What	**g**	Ken Sato.
8	What's your	**h**	action movies.

7 Choose the correct options to complete the sentences.

1 When you introduce yourself in writing, the first thing you tell the other person is ____.
   a your school   **b** your name   **c** your city

2 The second thing you write is ____.
   a what you enjoy   **b** how you feel   **c** where you're from

3 ____ usually tell each other what year they are in at school.
   a Students   **b** Teachers   **c** Classmates

4 In a new paragraph, you should write about ____.
   a your classmates   **b** the weather   **c** your hobbies

5 It's polite to ask the other person some questions about ____.
   a their interests   **b** their grades   **c** their problems

6 ____ by telling the other person that you look forward to hearing from him or her.
   a Start   **b** Finish   **c** Learn

8 Read the postcard to a student in California. Then read the questions and circle the answers in the postcard.

Dear Julie,

My name is Ana Cristina. I'm from Mexico City. It's a big and busy place! I'm in year 10 at secondary school.

At school, my favourite subjects are history and English. In my free time, I play the piano and I love singing songs in English. I'm also really into music festivals.

What about you? Do you play any instruments? Who is your favourite singer?

I look forward to hearing from you, Julie.

Best wishes,
Ana Cristina

1 What is the name of the person introducing herself?
2 Where is she from?
3 What year is she in at school?
4 What are her favourite subjects?
5 What instrument does she play?
6 What language does she like to sing in?
7 What else is she into?
8 She asks Julie about playing an instrument and what else?

9 Complete the postcard from Charlie to Amir. Write one word in each gap.

Dear Amir,

My _____ is Charlie Ford. I'm _____ Vancouver in Canada. I'm a _____ in grade 8.

My favourite _____ are geography and physics. I _____ the guitar, but I'm not very good! I _____ travelling to new places and I'm also _____ into video games.

What _____ you, Amir? Are you _____ video games, too? What are your favourite subjects at school?

I look forward to _____ from you.

Best regards,
Charlie

10 Read the profile. Imagine you are Alex Green and write a postcard introducing yourself.

PROFILE
Who:	*Alex Green*
What:	*Secondary school student, year 10*
Where:	*Edinburgh, UK*
Favourite subjects:	*chemistry and economics*
Musical instruments:	*none*
Hobbies:	*web design and hockey*

1	Include your name and other information.	*Dear _____,* *[Paragraph 1]*
2	Write about your favourite subjects and your hobbies.	*[Paragraph 2]*
3	Ask the other person some questions.	*[Paragraph 3]*
4	Write six sentences.	
5	Use some of the phrases you learned in this unit.	*I look forward to hearing from you.* *Best wishes,* *Alex*

Review

1 Circle eight adjectives that describe what people think about the singer.

Angélique Kidjo is a popular African singer and songwriter. She is from Benin, a small country in West Africa. She wears her hair very short and blonde. She's small, not tall, but she has a lot of personality! She's very cool and confident. She's very active. She travels a lot to perform her shows around the world. Angélique is talented, intelligent, kind and helpful. She started an organization, the Batonga Foundation, to help African women and girls get an education.

Angélique Kidjo

2 Match the sentences.

1 Angélique Kidjo is talented.	**a** Education is important to her.
2 She is popular.	**b** She helps women and girls in Africa.
3 She's very active.	**c** She's calm, not nervous, in front of people.
4 She's kind.	
5 She's intelligent.	**d** She's a great singer and songwriter.
6 She's confident.	**e** Many people like her.
	f She travels and performs a lot.

3 Correct the mistakes in the verb forms.

1 Sofia and her friends are liking _____ going shopping together at the weekend.

2 They going _____ to the shopping centre almost every Saturday afternoon.

3 They are often seeing _____ their friends from school there.

4 Filipe always buying _____ clothes or books.

5 Sofia often is looking _____ at the latest mobile phones.

6 Right now, Nele and Sofia drink _____ coffee and chatting.

7 They don't wanting _____ to see a film with Filipe.

8 Sometimes they are forgetting _____ where the car is because the car park is so big.

4 Choose the correct words to complete the sentences.

1 I _____ the instructions for the exam.
 a am reading   **c** doesn't read
 b is reading   **d** don't reading

2 She _____ a newspaper every morning.
 a buy   **c** is buying
 b doesn't buying   **d** buys

3 They _____ computer class today.
 a has   **c** doesn't have
 b don't have   **d** having

4 Are you _____ the piano?
 a practise   **c** doesn't practise
 b is practising   **d** practising

5 My aunt is a pilot. She _____ a plane.
 a don't fly   **c** fly
 b flies   **d** flying

6 _____ they rent an apartment in the city?
 a Doing   **c** Do
 b Does   **d** Doesn't

7 We never _____ in the sea.
 a swim   **c** do swim
 b are swimming   **d** swims

5 Use the prompts to write sentences and questions with the verb + -ing or the infinitive with to. Some sentences or questions have more than one correct answer.

1 I / would like / buy / a new jacket

_____.

2 They / usually / like / talk online

_____.

3 She / hate / shop for clothes

_____.

4 Do / you / like / help / your sister / learn English

_____?

5 What / he / want / read / before bed

_____?

6 I / want / tell you / about the end of the film

_____.

2A Different places

VOCABULARY Describing where you live

1 Revision Complete the sentences with the correct words.

apartment	bathroom	bedroom	city
kitchen	quiet	wall	

1 There's a clock on the _____ in our classroom.

2 I don't live in a house. I live in a(n) _____.

3 My flatmate is sleeping in his _____.

4 The food is in the _____.

5 I don't live in a small town. I live in the _____.

6 My street is busy. It's not _____.

7 We have a great new shower in our _____.

2 Revision Complete the text with the correct words.

bathrooms	bed	bedroom	dining room
garden	kitchen	living room	walls

My family moved into a new house two months ago. So far, I love it. The only problem is that the **(1)** _____ are all white. It's a bit boring. We want to paint them different colours!

My favourite room is the **(2)** _____ because I love to cook! We usually eat there, too. There's also a big **(3)** _____ in the house, but we only eat there when we invite friends to dinner.

I spend a lot of time in the **(4)** _____, where I read or watch TV.

I sleep well at night because my **(5)** _____ is at the back of the house, away from the street, so it's very quiet. Also, my **(6)** _____ is soft and comfortable!

There are two **(7)** _____, which is great. One is upstairs and one is downstairs. When someone is taking a shower upstairs, I don't have to wait for them to finish. I can just use the one downstairs!

Finally, there's also a big **(8)** _____ at the back of the house. It's beautiful. There are lots of trees and flowers.

3 Label the photos with the correct words.

chairs	decorations	a door	a light	a refrigerator
a sofa	stairs	a table	a window	

1 _____

2 _____

3 _____

4 _____

5 _____

6 _____

7 _____

8 _____

9 _____

4 Complete the sentences with the correct words.

1 Please open the w_____. It's hot in here.
2 You have to put the milk in the r_____.
3 The whole family is sitting on the s_____ and watching a film.
4 You can put the flowers in a vase on the dining room t_____.
5 The young girl has large photos of cute animals as a_____ in her bedroom.
6 There are a lot of s_____ because the house has four floors.
7 The d_____ to the bathroom is closed. Is someone in there?
8 The l_____ are off and the house is dark. Everyone is sleeping.

5 Match the words with the definitions.

1 urban
2 walkable
3 business district
4 traditional
5 modern
6 historic
7 suburban
8 shopping district
9 crowded
10 residential area
11 lively

a a place where there are a lot of office buildings
b not quiet or boring
c not old-fashioned
d a place where there are a lot of houses or apartments
e an area that people visit when they want to buy things
f not too far; safe for people travelling on foot
g full of people
h from an important time in the past
i not rural
j in an area outside a city
k an old way of doing things

6 Choose the correct words to complete the sentences.

1 Madrid is very *residential / lively* at night. Many people go out and they stay out very late.
2 Tokyo is a *crowded / rural* city, with a population of almost 38 million.
3 In Oaxaca, Mexico, you can eat many *traditional / walkable* foods such as *tlayudas* and *tamales*.
4 Lined with expensive stores and restaurants, the Champs-Élysées in Paris is one of the most famous *shopping / residential* districts in the world.
5 Ho-Ho-Kus, New Jersey, is a quiet *urban / suburban* town near New York City.
6 York is a beautiful *old-fashioned / historic* city in the UK with Roman walls and many old buildings.

7 If you like *modern / historic* buildings, then you should visit the 306-metre-high Cayan Tower in Dubai.

7 Listen and choose the correct description for each place. 🎧 14

1 a It's modern.
  b It's walkable.
  c It's crowded.
2 a It's the shopping district.
  b It's a residential area.
  c It's very lively.
3 a The area is very walkable.
  b It's a rural area.
  c It's the historic part of town.
4 a There's no furniture.
  b It's a very small apartment.
  c It's a traditional house.
5 a It's a historic area.
  b It's very modern.
  c It's a lively shopping district.
6 a It's a business.
  b It's a modern house.
  c It's old-fashioned.

8 Extension Fill in the missing vowels to form more words for things in a house or building.

1 __ v __ n
2 c __ pb __ __ rd
3 c __ b __ n __ t
4 c __ rp __ t
5 fl __ __ r
6 c __ sh __ __ n
7 b __ __ ksh __ lf
8 c __ __ l __ ng
9 s __ nk
10 c __ rt __ __ ns
11 t __ __ l __ t
12 w __ rdr __ b __
13 t __ p
14 dr __ w __ r

9 Extension Complete the text with the correct words.

carpets	ceiling	cupboards	curtains
drive	floor	sinks	toilet
traditional			

There is an upside-down house in Moscow that is not a **(1)** _____ house! There, the lights are on the **(2)** _____ and all the furniture and the **(3)** _____ are on the **(4)** _____. The **(5)** _____ hang from the 'bottom' of the windows instead of the 'top'. Cups and plates are upside-down inside the kitchen **(6)** _____. Even the car on the **(7)** _____ is upside-down! The **(8)** _____ in the kitchen and the bathroom can't work because the water would go in the wrong direction. And there isn't any water in the **(9)** _____ – it would fall out!

PRONUNCIATION /zd/ and /st/ in *used*

10 Read the sentences aloud. Circle the pronunciation of *use to*, *used to* or *used*. Listen and check your answers. 🎧 **15**

1 Finding an apartment used to be a lot easier.
  a /juːzd/   **b** /juːst/

2 Didn't you use to live in London?
  a /juːzd/   **b** /juːst/

3 They used all recycled materials to build the house.
  a /juːzd/   **b** /juːst/

4 Did you use to live in an apartment?
  a /juːzd/   **b** /juːst/

5 He used a lot of bamboo to build the house.
  a /juːzd/   **b** /juːst/

6 The city used to be a lot less crowded.
  a /juːzd/   **b** /juːst/

LISTENING

11 Listen and decide if each sentence is a fact (F) or an opinion (O). 🎧 **16**

1 _____   5 _____
2 _____   6 _____
3 _____   7 _____
4 _____   8 _____

12 Listen and tick the topics the speaker talks about. 🎧 **17**

1 construction materials _____
2 the Amazon _____
3 pollution _____
4 saving forests _____
5 cutting down and planting _____
6 hunting animals _____
7 recycling _____
8 the future of our planet _____

13 Listen again and answer the questions. 🎧 **17**

1 What is the gist or central idea of what the speaker is talking about?
  a the need to replace all forests with bamboo
  b reducing construction to protect the trees
  c only building with bamboo in the future
  d important ways to protect our forests

2 What adjective does she use meaning *to not think about the future*?
  a thoughtless   **c** old-fashioned
  b short-sighted   **d** traditional

3 What word does she use to describe a new tree?
  a seedling   **c** replacement
  b baby   **d** harvesting

4 What does she say about bamboo?
  a It's very inexpensive.
  b It doesn't grow in a forest.
  c It grows very quickly.
  d It can't be recycled.

5 What else does she talk about protecting?
  a seeds   **c** rivers
  b air   **d** animals

6 What do you think the speaker is trying to do?
  a persuade people not to use wood or paper products
  b convince people to be careful about what they use and buy
  c get people to stop using bamboo construction materials
  d encourage people to only cut down new seedlings to protect the forests

14 Listen and answer the questions. 🎧 **18**

1 How would you describe this young woman?
  a crazy
  b thoughtful
  c selfish

2 Who cares more about the effects of pollution?
  a the young woman
  b her colleague
  c both of them

3 What do you imagine is more important to the young woman?
  a a new car
  b good public transport
  c inexpensive taxis

4 What negative things does she mention about getting a car?
  a traffic, pollution and safety
  b cost, parking and pollution
  c parking, traffic and insurance

5 Which statement describes her attitude?
  a She doesn't care about her quality of life.
  b She only cares about others' quality of life.
  c She cares about everyone's quality of life.

6 What saying do you think she would agree with more?
  a We're all in this together.
  b You worry about your life and let me worry about mine.
  c You can never have enough.

GRAMMAR Past simple

15 Write the missing present simple or past simple form for each verb.

Present simple	Past simple	Present simple	Past simple
are			looked
	became	make	
change			moved
fly		see	
	went		spoke
grow		take	
	had	think	
	lived		worked

16 Choose the correct verb forms to complete the text.

My mother and I *need / am needing / needs* to find a new place to live. We *work / worked / are working* with an estate agent to find a new house. We *see / are seeing / saw* three different houses yesterday. The first one *not is / was / weren't* in a quiet area and *had / have / is having* a big kitchen and three bedrooms. But it *costed / cost / costing* too much for us. The second one *be / was / are* really cheap, but it *was / are / being* ugly and too far from my school. The third house *is having / had / have* lots of large windows and *is getting / get / got* lots of light. We *decided / are deciding / decide* to take that one because it *were / was / being* also near to where my mother works. We *plan / are planning / planning* to move in next month!

17 Complete the sentences with the past simple form of the verbs in brackets.

1 Before we _____ (move) here, we _____ (live) in a suburb far from the city.
2 Back then, my brother and I _____ (go) to school in the city. We _____ (take) a bus from our town into the city.
3 Our parents _____ (work) in the city and _____ (drive) to work every day.
4 Eventually, all of us _____ (become) tired of it because we _____ (spend) so much time commuting.
5 My parents _____ (decide) it would be better if we _____ (move) to the city.
6 At first, I _____ (think) this was a bad idea because I _____ (not, want) to leave my friends.

7 I _____ (be) afraid of not having friends and being lonely in the big city.
8 But I _____ (change) my mind when I _____ (realize) that my friends want to visit me here in the city!

18 Write a question for each answer.

1 _____ ?
  I walked to the cinema and met my friends there.
2 _____ ?
  He didn't go to the concert yesterday. It was on Friday.
3 _____ ?
  Yes, I think cities need green spaces and public parks.
4 _____ ?
  We lived in a city and walked everywhere.
5 _____ ?
  We didn't want to live in a historic house because it cost too much to maintain.
6 _____ ?
  My friend's house had a large swimming pool and a big garden.

19 Complete the sentences with the correct form of *use to*.

1 I _____ watch a lot of TV when I was younger, but now I don't.
2 I never _____ watch films on my computer, but now I do.
3 Like lots of kids, I _____ want to be an astronaut. Now I want to be a lawyer.
4 My sister didn't _____ like vegetables, but now she's a vegetarian!
5 Our cat _____ stay inside, but now he goes outside every day.
6 I _____ play games on my computer like my friends, but now I do.
7 What kind of games _____ you _____ play as a child?
8 I didn't _____ study every day, but now I do and my marks are much better!
9 Where _____ your grandparents _____ go to school when they were young?

2B My space

VOCABULARY BUILDING Suffix -ion

1 Complete each sentence with the noun form of the verb in brackets.

1 Did you send Max an _____ (invite) to the party?
2 The _____ (explore) of North America didn't begin with Columbus.
3 The detectives did a thorough _____ (investigate) of the crime scene.
4 What's the _____ (locate) of that restaurant?
5 My parents think it's very important to get a good _____ (educate).
6 The café is near the station – we're walking in the wrong _____ (direct)!

READING

2 Match the definitions with words from the text. There are two words you don't need.

1 an area marked for a specific purpose
2 the customary way of doing things
3 easy to get around on foot
4 the ability to form new ideas and see things that aren't real yet
5 suitable for living in
6 referring to the city instead of the countryside
7 where people work, buy and sell goods and services

a business
b walkable
c district
d imagination
e modern
f residential
g transportation
h traditional
i urban

3 Read the text again. Are the sentences true (T), false (F) or is the information not given (NG)?

1 Floating cities are home to 7 billion people. _____
2 Over 100,000 people could live in a Green Float city. _____
3 A floating Lilypad city would be completely self-sufficient. _____
4 Each Lilypad would contain around 50,000 homes. _____
5 Floating cities like Lilypad only exist on paper. _____
6 Coastal cities may someday be threatened by flooding. _____

4 Choose the correct heading for each paragraph.

Paragraph 1:
  a Where will we live in the future?
  b Would you like to live in a city?

Paragraph 2:
  a Designing a new type of city
  b People all over the world are building new ships and cities

Paragraph 3:
  a An underwater farm
  b Another type of floating city

Paragraph 4:
  a Inventors and their imaginations
  b Why floating cities matter

5 Read and choose the correct options.

1 According to the information in paragraph 2, it is <u>not</u> true that
  a people are thinking about developing cities on the ocean.
  b the first floating cities will be near Brazil.
  c a Japanese company is working on a floating city idea.
  d the plans for Green Float include walkable neighbourhoods.

2 Why does the author mention Lilypad's sources of energy?
  a to show that it is self-sufficient
  b to explain why there are no cars
  c to contrast it with the energy sources of Green Float
  d to give an example of farming below the water

3 Why does the author say floating cities 'only exist on paper'?
  a Floating cities appear on maps of the Pacific Ocean.
  b Only 100,000 people can live in a floating city.
  c Floating cities don't exist yet.
  d They are in science-fiction stories.

4 In the article, the word *inventors* in paragraph 4 is closest in meaning to
  a residents.
  b builders.
  c creators.
  d instructors.

Floating cities of the future

1 🎧 **19** We all know that the ocean covers a large part of the Earth's surface. We also know that with 7 billion people on this planet, space for housing is running out! Where do you want to live in the future? In a city? Near the ocean? How about a city in the ocean?

2 In the past, people thought that floating cities were only in science-fiction stories. Today, people are developing plans for new types of buildings and cities, including some that float on the surface* of the ocean. Japan's Shimizu Corporation is working on a 'Green Float' idea. The company wants to build a floating city in the Pacific Ocean. And just like the cities we know today, the plan for Green Float's city on the ocean includes residential areas, shopping districts, walkable neighbourhoods and business districts.

3 Another plan for a floating city takes its name and inspiration from a plant. An architect designed Lilypad to be an ecologically friendly, ultra-modern city that's completely self-sufficient*. A Lilypad city gets energy from the sun, wind and the ocean's tide. Boats and other floating vehicles are the only transportation for the 50,000 future residents of a Lilypad.

4 Today, cities like the Lilypads only exist on paper and in the imaginations of their inventors. But these new ideas for housing are important for the future. Traditional ways of living need to change. Major

Lilypad

urban centres are becoming more and more crowded every day. Floating cities are one possible answer to the need for more housing.

surface *the top of something*
self-sufficient *able to provide for its needs*

2C A unique style

GRAMMAR Past continuous

1 Read the paragraph. Circle the past continuous verbs.

When I went to Prague last year, I was planning to visit historic buildings and I did. But I was not expecting to see a historic lift. This unusual lift was running nonstop! It also didn't have doors! People stepped into the lift as it was moving up or down. I was thinking how unsafe it was when the tour guide told us the name. It's called a *paternoster* after a prayer that people said as they rode it. People prayed because the lift was dangerous. The guide explained that the lift was working like a Ferris wheel, moving people up and down in a circle. The important thing about riding the *paternoster* was making sure that you got off before it reached the top and turned over to go back down.

Ferris wheel

2 Read about Raul's day. Complete the sentences using the past continuous.

> 7:00–8:30 exercised at the gym
>
> 8:45–9:15 had breakfast with his uncle
>
> 9:15–9:45 took the bus to school
>
> 10:00–10:30 met with his study group
>
> 10:30–12:15 studied in the library
>
> 12:15–12:45 ate lunch with his friend David
>
> 1:00–2:15 attended his English class

1 At 8:15, Raul _____was exercising at the gym_____.
2 At 9:00, Raul _____.
3 At 9:30, Raul _____.
4 At 10:15, Raul _____.
5 At 11:00, Raul _____.
6 At 12:30, Raul _____.
7 At 1:45, Raul _____.

3 Choose the correct words to complete the sentences.

1 Hana *arrived / was arriving* an hour early for her flight to Seoul.
2 I *relaxed / was relaxing* at home when I got a call from my boss.
3 I saw Raj at the Student Union and *asked / was asking* him if he had time to help me prepare for my maths exam.
4 Pedro *listened / was listening* to music when suddenly the power went off.
5 Last night, my sister *cleaned / was cleaning* up the kitchen after dinner.
6 Congratulations on your new job! I *heard / was hearing* the good news last week.
7 I *saw / was seeing* him walk past my office on his way to the meeting.
8 The taxi came much too early; we *ate / were eating* breakfast when it arrived.

4 Complete the sentences using the past continuous or past simple form of the verb in brackets.

1 The bus drove by while we _____ (walk) to school.
2 I looked out the window and _____ (notice) it was snowing.
3 After Kira _____ (make) breakfast, she washed the dishes.
4 She _____ (ask) me to help her move into her new house.
5 She _____ (play) football with her friends, but had to stop to take her little brother to his piano lesson.
6 I _____ (meet) Antonio at the party last night.
7 Elena wrote a letter to her grandmother last week, but _____ (forget) to send it.
8 I _____ (watch) TV when I heard the news.

5 Use the prompts to write sentences with the past continuous and past simple. Add any necessary words.

1 I / do the laundry / while / my mother / make dinner
2 I / make lunch / when / my phone / ring
3 she / fall off / while / ride bike
4 we / run / down the street / when / bus / leave the station
5 Claire / shop / new sofa / when / find / great sale
6 while / they / save money / a new house, / win the lottery

7 Jaime / read book / when / mum / call

8 I / break / laptop / while / play / new game

6 Complete the conversation with the past continuous of the verbs in brackets.

Chimneys on the roof of Casa Milà

A Hey, Julia! Welcome back! **(1)** _Were you travelling_ (travel) last term?

B Yes, I was. I **(2)** _____ (study) in Barcelona.

A That is so cool! Where **(3)** _____ (live)?

B I **(4)** _____ (live) in this really cool neighbourhood called the Eixample. It's pretty famous for its architecture. It's a nice area – residential, but there is still a lot of shopping and restaurants. Do you know it?

A Yeah, I do. Is that where Antoni Gaudí **(5)** _____ (work) in the late 1800s?

B Yes! His buildings are so amazing! I **(6)** _____ (stay) in a house just two blocks away from Casa Milà, a famous apartment building he designed.

A You're so lucky! I **(7)** _____ (hope) to visit Barcelona when I went to Spain last year, but I ran out of time.

B Well, I'm sure you **(8)** _____ (enjoy) yourself in other places.

A Yeah, but I **(9)** _____ (hear) so many great things about the parks and monuments in Barcelona from everyone! Now, **(10)** _____ Gaudí _____ (not build) something when he died? A church?

B Yes, he **(11)** _____ (work) on a large cathedral, the _Sagrada Familia_. It still isn't finished, but the city **(12)** _____ (work) on it when I left!

7 Choose the option which is closer in meaning to the original sentence.

1 I was listening to my brother telling me about his day when someone rang the doorbell.
   a I started listening to my brother. Then someone rang the doorbell.
   b The doorbell rang. Then I started listening to my brother.

2 He was eating lunch outside because it had stopped raining.
   a It stopped raining. Then he ate lunch outside.
   b He ate lunch outside. Then it stopped raining.

3 Sam was practising the trumpet when he suddenly heard his flatmate asking him for help.
   a Sam's flatmate asked for help before Sam practised the trumpet.
   b Sam's flatmate asked for help while Sam was practising the trumpet.

4 She hurt her leg while she was playing basketball.
   a When she hurt her leg, she played basketball.
   b When she was playing basketball, she hurt her leg.

5 Before I moved to Tokyo, I was living in Amsterdam.
   a I lived in Amsterdam. Then I lived in Tokyo.
   b I moved to Tokyo. Then I lived in Amsterdam.

6 Yesterday, Beatrix was listening to music while she cleaned her apartment.
   a Beatrix started listening to music. Then she cleaned her apartment.
   b Beatrix listened to music and cleaned her apartment at the same time.

7 I was thinking about going back to school, but decided to take a new job instead.
   a I went back to school and also took a new job.
   b I thought about going back to school, but I didn't.

8 Choose the correct response for each question.

1 Did you read _Animal Farm_ when you were in secondary school?
   a Yes, we read it in year nine.
   b Yes, we were reading it in year nine.

2 Where were you when I tried to call you?
   a I talked to my mother.
   b I was talking to my mother.

3 Why did you call me?
   a I wanted to ask you about going walking next weekend.
   b I wanting to ask you about going walking next weekend.

4 Did you hear what I said?
   a No, sorry. I was concentrating on my work.
   b No, sorry. I concentrated on my work.

5 Where did you meet your friend Amy?
   a We were meeting at university.
   b We met at university.

6 Did they graduate in 2017?
   a No, they were graduating in 2016.
   b No, they graduated in 2016.

7 Where did you buy this comfortable chair?
   a I found it in a furniture shop near school.
   b I was finding it in a furniture shop near school.

8 What were you doing at 8:15 this morning?
   a I was exercising before I caught the bus to work at 9:30.
   b I caught the bus while I was exercising at 9:30.

2D Magical houses, made of bamboo

TEDTALKS

AUTHENTIC LISTENING SKILLS

1 Listen to the TED Talk extracts. Choose the correct answers. 🎧 20

1 What is this extract about?
 a the different homes in Bali
 b the homes Elora designed
 c different parts of any home

2 What is this extract about?
 a a special kind of bamboo
 b how her father builds with bamboo
 c how tall bamboo plants grow

3 What is this extract about?
 a trucks that go through mountains
 b the plants the family grows
 c a really strong bamboo

4 What is this extract about?
 a why bamboo is a good material
 b how the children study in Bali
 c how to stay safe in an earthquake

5 What is this extract about?
 a how to be an extraordinary person
 b how to be an architect
 c how to build something great with bamboo

WATCH ▶

2 Watch the TED Talk. Are the statements true (T) or false (F)?

1 Bamboo is a wild grass. _____
2 There are seven species of bamboo around the world. _____
3 Betung is as strong as steel. _____
4 Betung is so heavy that many people are needed to carry it. _____
5 Bamboo can be easily broken by earthquakes. _____
6 Bamboo is a material that is good for the environment.
 _____

3 Put the events in the correct order.

_____ Her father plants a bamboo called *Dendrocalamus asper niger*.

_____ Elora draws a picture of her dream home.

_____ Elora realizes how bamboo is important and thinks about what else she can do with it.

_____ Elora sees one of the buildings from the Green School in Bali.

_____ Her mother builds a home that looks like a fairy mushroom.

4 Choose the correct answers.

1 What is the speaker mainly discussing?
 a how she is a good home designer
 b why bamboo is a great material
 c the way everyone should build their homes

2 What does the speaker mean when she says this: 'Bamboo will treat you well if you use it right.'?
 a Bamboo has to be used carefully.
 b Bamboo can be used the same way by everyone.
 c Bamboo can take care of people.

3 What can be inferred about the speaker's father?
 a His main job is a farmer.
 b He builds homes and buildings like Elora.
 c He works for Elora.

4 Why does the speaker say: 'protect it (bamboo) from water'?
 a Water can make the bamboo grow bigger.
 b Water is not a good building material.
 c Water can be bad for bamboo when building.

5 Why does the speaker mention designing in 3D?
 a to explain how easy it is to design in 3D
 b to show how much planning she does before building
 c to give an example of the best way to design

6 What is a *blueprint*?
 a a piece of bamboo
 b a part of a home
 c a plan for a home

VOCABULARY IN CONTEXT

5 Match the expressions with the situations.

1 It didn't feel right.
2 I've got to tell you something.
3 It looks elegant.
4 It will treat you well.
5 It makes perfect sense.

a You see a stylish jacket and you really like it.
b When you take care of something and you expect it will be good to you.
c Someone tells you a good idea that solves your problems.
d Someone tells you to do something you aren't comfortable doing.
e When you learn exciting and new information you want to share.

6 Elora Hardy talks about designing houses for the tropics, where it can get very hot. Think about your home. Can you give an example of how it was designed for the place you live?

2E Special things, special places

SPEAKING

Useful language

Giving reasons

Use *The reason…*, *because*, *so* and *since* to give reasons.

The reason *he went there was to get away from his money problems.*

He went **because** *his business failed.*

She thought life was too hard, **so** *she left.*

Since *he loved living a simple life in a tiny house, he didn't want to leave.*

1 Complete the sentences with words from the Useful language box. Listen and check your answers. 🎧 **21**

  1 I used to spend a lot of time outside
  _____ I lived in a small apartment.

  2 _____ I went to Barcelona was to see the amazing architecture.

  3 My house is in the countryside, _____ I spend a lot of time by myself.

  4 _____ I have four brothers and sisters, our place was very noisy.

2 Think about some things you don't do and the reasons why. Complete the sentences about yourself.

  Examples:
  Since I don't like shopping, *I* don't go to shopping centres very much.

  I don't enjoy swimming, *so I* don't often visit our local pool.

  1 The reason I don't _____
  _____ is to
  _____.

  2 Since I don't _____
  _____,
  I _____.

  3 I don't _____,
  so _____.

  4 I don't _____
  because _____.

3 You're designing a dream house. Look at the options in the box and choose four to include in your design, or use your own ideas. Use the prompts to explain reasons for your choices. Use the Useful language.

a garden	bamboo
big windows	energy-saving lights
lots of indoor plants	solar panels
swimming pool	walkable neighbourhood

  1 The first thing the dream house needs is _____
  _____
  _____
  _____
  _____.

  2 It's also important that the house have _____
  _____
  _____
  _____
  _____.

  3 Another thing it should have is _____
  _____
  _____
  _____
  _____.

  4 Finally, I think _____ is/are very important.
  _____
  _____
  _____
  _____.

After you complete the sentences, listen to the model answers and compare them with your answers. 🎧 **22**

4 Answer the questions and give reasons for your ideas, using the Useful language. Then listen to the model answers and compare them with your ideas. 🎧 **23**

  1 Do you prefer spending your free time at home or going out?
  2 Tell me a little about your hometown.
  3 What did you like about where you lived as a child?
  4 What do you do in your free time in your hometown?

WRITING A description

5 Match the questions with the answers.

1 Where is it?
2 When did you go there?
3 How old is it?
4 What does it look like?
5 Who lives there?
6 What did you see or do there?

a It's a huge house with beautiful gardens and views of New York City.
b I really enjoyed visiting the art gallery on the first floor of the house.
c My favourite house is in Westchester County, New York.
d The house is more than 100 years old. It was built in 1913.
e A few weeks ago, my aunt and uncle took me to visit this house.
f It's the home of a very rich American family called the Rockefellers.

6 Read the email and put the information in the correct order.

Hi Claire,

Glad you enjoyed your trip. I had a great time too.

I stayed in the most amazing apartment in Dubai. I went there a few months ago with my best friend, Amira, when we were on our way to Australia. It's only a few years old and it's definitely the most modern apartment I've ever seen. It has white walls and a huge balcony, and a swimming pool! It belongs to Amira's uncle, but he only lives there sometimes, because he travels a lot for business. When we were there, we swam in the pool every morning and drank tea on the balcony every evening. It was such a wonderful home to visit.

Laura

When Laura went there: _____
What she did there: _____
What it looks like: _____
Where it is: _____
How old it is: _____
Who lives there: _____

7 Complete the text with the correct words.

| designed | family | garden | gates |
| saw | special | tower | years |

I love the Gaudi House in Barcelona, which is in Catalonia. I went there on a trip with my **(1)** _____ last month. It's in Park Guell and it's now a museum. The house is about 100 **(2)** _____ old and it's amazing. One part has a tall **(3)** _____, which looks like a castle! It's pretty big, with four floors, many windows and huge **(4)** _____. It's **(5)** _____ because a famous architect, called Antoni Gaudi, lived there for almost twenty years.

He **(6)** _____ many incredible buildings in Barcelona, but not this house! When I went there, I **(7)** _____ lots of beautiful art and some strange furniture. After our visit, we had a picnic in the **(8)** _____. It was really nice.

Ken

8 Read the text in Exercise 7 again. Choose the correct options to complete the sentences.

1 The Gaudi House is in a city called *Barcelona / Catalonia*.
2 Ken went there last *year / month*.
3 The house is *100 / 20* years old.
4 Part of the house looks like a *museum / castle*.
5 The house is quite *small / large*.
6 A famous man called *Gaudi / Guell* used to live there.
7 The furniture that Ken saw there was *unusual / beautiful*.

9 Read the notes and imagine you visited the house in the photo. A friend has asked you about it. Write a paragraph (80–100 words) describing your visit. In your paragraph you should say:

• where it is and when you went there
• how old it is, its location and what's special about it
• who used to live in it, and what you did or saw there.

Notes about the house:
• in Ireland
• visited cousin there last summer
• house was built in 1757
• pretty cottage in the countryside
• very old furniture
• great-grandparents used to live there
• baked bread in the old oven

10 A teacher gave you an assignment to write a story. The first sentence of the story is: *The lighthouse where I stayed in Canada was the best house I have ever visited.* Write the story (100 words) in your notebook.

Review

1 Unscramble the letters to make words about furniture or items in a house.

1 arsist _____
2 scriha _____
3 fergritroare _____
4 orcastedino _____
5 blate _____
6 gilth _____
7 onwsdiw _____
8 afos _____

2 Choose the best option to complete each sentence.

1 The lift doesn't work, so we have to take the _____ up to our hotel room.
  a door   **b** stairs   **c** window

2 My aunt lives in a _____ house from the 1700s.
  a modern   **b** walkable   **c** historic

3 There are six _____ in the dining room – one for each dinner guest.
  a chairs   **b** tables   **c** sofas

4 His apartment is very plain and boring. He has basic furniture but no _____ at all.
  a lights   **b** refrigerators   **c** decorations

5 If a restaurant is always _____, that usually means the food is pretty good.
  a old-fashioned   **b** crowded   **c** traditional

6 Adrian and Martin _____ school last week.
  a studied   **b** went   **c** finished

3 Correct the mistakes in the conversations.

1 A When do you moved to your new apartment?
_____
  B I was move in last week. _____

2 A Do you saw anything interesting at the shops?
_____
  B No, I didn't saw anything new.
_____

3 A Did you took the metro to the train station?
_____
  B No. I taked the bus. It's faster. _____

4 A Did you drew this picture of your grandparents?
_____
  B Yes, I did. I drawed it last night.
_____

5 A I readed a good article in the sports magazine last night. _____
  B Really? Did you enjoyed it? _____

6 A I didn't used to like to dance, but now I love it!
_____
  B Really? What change your mind?
_____

4 Complete the table.

Infinitive	Past simple	Past continuous
grow	*grew*	*was/were growing*
watch		
dance		
make		
buy		
fly		
leave		
ride		
travel		
become		
live		
think		

5 Complete the sentences based on the information provided.

1 I ate lunch before you called.
I _____ lunch when you called.

2 He took English classes. During one of those classes, he decided to study in Australia.
While he _____ English classes, he _____ to study in Australia.

3 They fell asleep before the train stopped.
They _____ when the train _____.

4 I think I remember you went shopping for a new wallet.
_____ you _____ to find a new wallet?

5 I looked for a new wallet at the shopping centre. While I was at the shopping centre, I found a wallet I wanted to buy.
I _____ for a new wallet and finally _____ one at the shopping centre.

6 We talked about our friend Ana at the same time as we rode our bikes to the pool.
We _____ our bikes to the pool while we _____ about our friend Ana.

7 You studied for the exam. I want to know if your sisters bothered you then.
_____ your sisters _____ you while you _____ for the exam?

3A Treating the whole person

VOCABULARY Being well

1 **Revision** Choose the correct words to complete the sentences.

1 You see with your _____.
   a eyes   **b** teeth

2 Your back is part of your _____.
   a body   **b** face

3 When your tooth hurts, you go to the _____.
   a doctor   **b** dentist

4 When you catch a cold, you feel _____.
   a fine   **b** ill

5 When you don't feel well, you go to the _____.
   a doctor   **b** dentist

6 You usually recognize someone by looking at their _____.
   a back   **b** face

7 Smoking isn't good _____.
   a to you   **b** for you

2 **Revision** Listen and match the descriptions with the images. 🎧 24

a
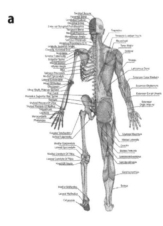

b

c
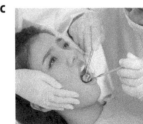

d
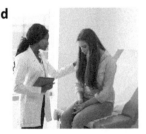

e

f

g

h

1 _____   4 _____   7 _____
2 _____   5 _____   8 _____
3 _____   6 _____

3 Put the words into the correct category.

| backache | chest | flu | foot | mouth |
| pain | seasickness | shoulder | stomach | virus |

Body part	Illness

4 Write the correct words.

1 _____   5 _____
2 _____   6 _____
3 _____   7 _____
4 _____   8 _____

5 Complete the text with the correct words. There are two words you don't need.

broken	happiness	healthy	hospital
illnesses	injuries	medicine	pain
patient	unwell	viruses	

We all know that laughing makes us feel good – in fact, there is a saying that 'laughter is the best
(1) _____.' Positive thoughts and happy feelings can certainly take some of our
(2) _____ away. But many scientists and doctors believe there is an even stronger connection between **(3)** _____ and health. Some studies show that happier people heal faster after
(4) _____ such as a
(5) _____ leg. They also show that positive feelings can help prepare your body to fight
(6) _____ better. On the other hand, negative feelings like stress can lead to
(7) _____ such as heart disease and diabetes over time. In short, happier people are more likely to be **(8)** _____ and make fewer visits to
(9) _____.

6 Listen and match the topics (1–6) with the talks (a–f)
🎧 **25**

1 a common virus _____
2 seasickness _____
3 a problem with a pain medicine _____
4 patients who get more unwell instead of better _____
5 reading people's faces and body language _____
6 sports injuries _____

7 Extension Where is it? Choose the correct answer for each body part.

1 brain
  a inside the head
  b inside the chest

2 finger
  a part of the foot
  b part of the hand

3 toe
  a part of the foot
  b part of the face

4 cheek
  a below the neck
  b part of the face

5 wrist
  a part of your arm
  b part of your leg

6 chin
  a inside the body
  b you can see it

7 bones
  a inside the body
  b you can see them

8 lungs
  a inside the body
  b you can see them

9 ankles
  a inside the body
  b you can see them

10 blood
  a on your face
  b in your whole body

8 Extension Complete the sentences with the correct words.

accident	ankles	blood	bone	brain	chin
heart	lungs	recover	toe	wrists	

1 Your _____ thinks and controls everything in your body.
2 Your _____ is inside your chest and it pumps _____ around your body.
3 Your _____ are also inside your chest. They take air in and push it out.
4 If you have a/an _____, you could break a/an _____ in your leg or your arm.
5 It's very painful to hit your big _____ on a table when you walk into it.
6 Your forehead and your _____ are both parts of your face.
7 Your _____ help you move your hands. Your _____ help you move your feet.
8 When you _____ from an illness or injury, you get better.

9 Extension Choose the correct words to complete the text.

In 2013, motorcyclist Nick Matthews had a terrible *blood / accident*. His neck was broken and his *back / heart* was broken in three places. He also had a broken *wrist / cheek*, two broken *fingers / brains* and several broken *bones / ankles* in his chest area. To make matters worse, he had a serious *lung / chin* injury, which caused him to stop breathing. In the hospital, the doctors thought he might not walk again. But three weeks later, Matthews walked out of hospital. He *recovered / injured* completely and ran in the Berlin Marathon, just one year later!

PRONUNCIATION Contrastive stress

10 Listen and choose the stressed word or phrase. 🎧 26

1 **a** you said
  b a few
  c problems

2 **a** no
  b knee
  c neck

3 **a** How much
  b you
  c it costs

4 **a** kind
  b mind
  c matter

5 **a** biggest
  b problem
  c world

6 **a** kidding me
  b call
  c a little

LISTENING

11 Listen and choose the illness or injury in the description. 🎧 27

1 **a** the flu
  b a broken hand
  c an earache

2 **a** a broken nose
  b a bad cold
  c backache

3 **a** a shoulder injury
  b a knee injury
  c a headache

4 **a** a broken temperature
  b a high temperature
  c a sore leg

5 **a** a neck injury
  b a nose injury
  c a knee injury

6 **a** the flu
  b seasickness
  c a broken leg

7 **a** seasickness
  b a headache
  c the flu

12 Listen. What is the speaker mainly talking about? 🎧 28

a People who go to the doctor and take medicine are sensitive.
b Medical professionals don't believe in mind over matter.
c The mind-body connection is important in understanding health.
d Meditation is better than visiting a doctor or taking medicine.

13 Listen again and choose the correct answers to the questions. 🎧 28

1 What phrasal verb does the speaker use meaning to *handle* or *manage*?
  a take control
  b deal with
  c depend on
  d look after

2 What adjective does the speaker use for people who don't handle pain well?
  a anxious
  b serious
  c stressful
  d sensitive

3 What phrasal verb does the speaker use meaning to *stop* or *end*?
  a cut off
  b take out
  c turn off
  d able to

4 What adjective does the speaker use to describe doctors?
  a prescription
  b professional
  c patient
  d serious

5 What two things are connected in the idea of mind over matter?
  a symptoms and pain
  b body and mind
  c patient and doctor
  d prescription medicine and meditation

6 According to the speaker, what can some people do that others can't?
  a tolerate pain
  b describe their symptoms
  c deal with their doctor
  d meditate

14 Listen. Are the sentences true (T) or false (F)? 🎧 29

1 She used to enjoy showing off her money and success. _____
2 She was very unhappy earlier in her life. _____
3 She was missing the company of close friends. _____
4 She wasn't sure what was missing in her life. _____
5 She learned about Habitat for Humanity from a friend. _____
6 Habitat for Humanity charges a lot of money for their homes. _____
7 Her boss allowed her to take time off from work. _____
8 It's not certain that she will return to her old job. _____

A volunteer works on a house.

GRAMMAR Quantifiers, *how much / many?*

15 Put the words into the correct category.

air	arm	ear	exercise
eye	the flu	hand	health
hospital	injury	leg	medicine
patient	skin	water	

Countable	Uncountable

16 Choose the correct options to complete the sentences.

1 My doctor gave me _____ really good suggestions for things I can do to get back into shape.
   a some
   b any

2 She told me that I should do _____ exercise every couple of hours – just a few minutes is enough.
   a a few
   b a little

3 She said that _____ people think they have to go to the gym to exercise, but you can do some exercises at home without expensive equipment.
   a a lot of
   b a little

4 For _____ of the exercises, you can use the weight of your body.
   a much
   b many

5 The intensity of the exercise depends on how _____ you weigh.
   a many
   b much

6 Another tip from my doctor was to drink _____ water throughout the day.
   a a lot of
   b a few

7 And to eat _____ grapes as a snack rather than crisps or biscuits.
   a a little
   b a few

17 Complete the questions and statements with *how much* or *how many*.

1 _____ time do you spend at the gym?
2 _____ times do you meditate each week?

3 _____ medicine do you take every day?
4 _____ pills do you take at breakfast?
5 _____ did you weigh the last time you went to the doctor?
6 I don't know _____ times I was ill last year.
7 My doctor told me _____ sleep I should get every night.
8 No one knows _____ people have the flu each year.

18 Complete the sentences with the correct words. In some sentences there may be more than one correct answer.

| a little | any | many | much |
| not any | not much | some | |

1 I still have _____ pain in my shoulder after working on the house.
2 The doctor told me I still have _____ more weight to lose.
3 Do your grandparents take _____ pills to keep themselves well?
4 We didn't have _____ junk food in our house, so we had to eat fruit.
5 The coach showed us _____ really fun exercises you can do with a chair.
6 Do you have _____ bandages? I cut my finger and it's bleeding.
7 The doctors do _____ have _____ idea how long the illness will last.
8 We do _____ have _____ food in the house, so we should go to the supermarket.

19 Correct the quantifier in each sentence.

1 Last night, I went to the hospital because I had much pain in my stomach. _____
2 I don't know how much hours I waited there, but I finally saw the doctor around midnight. _____
3 She asked me how many pain I had. _____
4 I told her there was a few pain in my stomach and that I could barely walk. _____
5 She asked me if I ate too many food at dinner. _____
6 I told her that I ate too many pizza and then I ate a big bowl of ice cream. _____
7 She asked me a lot of slices of pizza and I told her, 'Six.' _____
8 She said I was in pain because I ate too many food! _____
9 I won't eat so many pizza or ice cream ever again! _____

3B Painless

VOCABULARY BUILDING Synonyms

1 Match the words or phrases with their synonyms.

1 happy   well
    healthy   sickness
    unwell   content
    illness   ill

2 discover   combine
    mix   find
    entire   whole
    think   believe

3 angry   try
    attempt   upset
    several   normal
    typical   some

READING

2 Read the text and choose the correct answers to the questions.

1 What do some people mean when they say that they want to 'go on a diet'?

   a They want to eat more grains and beans.

   b They mean more than one thing.

   c They want to eat every day.

   d They want to lose weight.

2 What can happen when you lose weight suddenly?

   a You skip a few meals every week.

   b Your body thinks there's a problem.

   c You eat more meat and fish.

   d Your body type varies.

3 What does Linda Bacon recommend that you do in order to stay healthy?

   a Eat less food and miss several meals a week.

   b Worry about whether you're too big or too small.

   c Move your body and try to find foods that you enjoy.

   d Keep eating even after you're full.

4 What is a 'diet'?

   a the food you normally eat

   b a fun physical activity

   c a type of exercise

   d a way to stay alert

5 According to HAES, what are two ways to avoid feeling unwell?

   a Go on a diet and lose weight suddenly.

   b Eat less and miss a few meals.

   c Eat good food and get physical activity.

   d Sleep a lot and worry about your weight.

3 Choose the correct words to complete the sentences.

1 It's important to be aware of what you _____ in order to stay healthy.

   a wear

   b eat

   c say

   d hear

2 Many people think that going on a diet is a good way to _____ weight.

   a avoid

   b recognize

   c lose

   d feel

3 Being aware of what you eat can help you avoid certain _____.

   a illnesses

   b diets

   c weight

   d hungry

4 HAES doesn't believe that everyone should be the same _____.

   a height

   b age

   c weight

   d way

5 In order to stay healthy, your body needs many different _____.

   a nutrients

   b experiments

   c mix

   d weights

4 Match the information (a–f) with the paragraphs (1–4). You may use numbers more than once.

   a recommendations for healthy eating and activities _____

   b two easy ways to avoid feeling unwell _____

   c a description of how bodies react to sudden weight loss _____

   d two definitions for the word *diet* _____

   e a description of how people vary physically _____

   f how listening to your body can help you feel well _____

Health at every size

1 🎧 30 The word *diet* can mean a couple of things. What you normally eat every day is your regular diet. If you eat meat or fish, grains or beans, fruit or vegetables, then those foods are part of your diet. But *diet* also has another meaning, one that you may be more familiar with. When people say that they want to 'go on a diet,' they usually mean that they want to lose some weight. They may think that by eating less, missing a few meals or eating only certain foods, they'll lose weight and become healthier.

2 Of course, everyone wants to stay healthy, avoid illnesses and live longer, but dieting isn't always the best way to do it! Like height or skin colour, weight and body type are different from person to person. A person's ideal weight range* is called their 'set-point' weight. When you go on a diet and lose weight quickly, your body thinks the sudden weight loss is a problem or challenge. It will do whatever it can to get you back to your set-point or average weight.

3 Health at Every Size (HAES) is a group that encourages healthy eating and fun physical activity as two easy ways to avoid feeling unwell and live longer. HAES doesn't believe weight loss through dieting is the way to become healthy. As Linda Bacon, a researcher and the author of *Health at every size: the surprising truth about your weight* says, 'Health at Every Size is about taking care of your body without worrying about whether you're 'too' big or small. Saying everybody needs to be the same weight is like saying all people should be the same height.'

4 'What's good for thin kids, fat kids and everyone in between, it turns out, is moving their bodies, and a healthy mix of foods that taste good and nourish their bodies. Finding the activities you enjoy might mean sports or workouts, but it could also be walking, jumping rope with friends or dancing,' Bacon says. She recommends trying out a variety of foods to find those that you enjoy most or make you happy (within reason – of course that doesn't mean you should eat a lot of junk food!). 'This means learning to listen to your body so you can recognize when you're hungry and when you're full, and what foods satisfy you. So mix it up and get a range of nutrients in you to keep you alert* and in a good mood. Experiment with food to see which ones make you feel best!'

range *the highest and lowest numbers in a series*
alert *paying attention; wide awake*

3C What makes us happy?

GRAMMAR Phrasal verbs

1 Put the phrasal verbs into the correct category.

belong to	bring back	carry out (do)
deal with	eat out	go in
keep up	look around	pick up
put on (music)	sit down	take off (clothing)
wake up	write down	

Separable	Inseparable

2 Complete the second sentence so that it means the same as the first. Use no more than three words.

1 He brought the book back to the library.

He _____ the book to the library.

2 She wrote her information on the application.

She _____ her information on the application.

3 He filled in the form and gave it to the teacher.

He filled in the form and _____.

4 She took off her hat.

She _____ off.

5 Please pass on the book after you read it.

Please _____ the book _____ after you read it.

6 Did you pick the coffee up on your way to work?

Did you _____ the coffee on your way to work?

7 I turned down the TV after my neighbour said it was too loud.

I _____ the TV _____ after my neighbour said it was too loud.

3 Choose the correct words to complete the sentences.

1 I handed it _____ last week.
   a in
   b on
   c with

2 How many times did you work _____ at the gym last week?
   a with
   b up
   c out

3 I wrote his name and phone number _____.
   a into
   b about
   c down

4 Please bring it _____ by Friday.
   a back
   b out
   c down

5 He looked _____ moving to Brazil.
   a back
   b into
   c off

6 I give _____! I just can't do it.
   a up
   b on
   c with

7 I was turning _____ the lights when my friend Luiz walked into the room.
   a back
   b on
   c in

8 Let's put the film _____ after we eat dinner.
   a on
   b out
   c into

9 Is your dad looking _____ your little brother today?
   a up
   b out
   c after

4 Match the two parts of the sentences.

1 You can't give
2 Did you hand
3 They're looking
4 Did he put
5 He's dealing
6 Please take
7 Were you hanging
8 Remember to turn

a out at the cinema last weekend?
b on the oven 30 minutes before you put in the pizza.
c in your homework on time?
d up – just keep trying!
e into getting someone to help around the house.
f with a lot of problems at work.
g on his new suit for the interview?
h out the rubbish before you leave.

5 Complete the sentences with the correct form of the phrasal verbs.

deal with	get along with	get on
give up	hang out	look after
put on	work out	

1 Hurry! _____ the train before it leaves.
2 Dina _____ her flatmate very well.
3 Francis likes to _____ at the beach every Saturday.
4 She _____ her sister before their mum gets home from work.
5 How do you _____ the stress of working and studying?
6 I told him he needs to _____ junk food.
7 Let's go to the gym and _____ today.
8 I was _____ my jacket when the phone rang.

6 Correct the sentences.

1 I picked my friend from the train station up.
_____

2 Let's hang into Gina and Ruby on Friday.
_____

3 Rae deals her pain with by doing yoga.
_____

4 Suneeta is looking in her neighbour's cat while he's on holiday.
_____

5 Please down sit.
_____

6 My mum left a voicemail message for me, so back her I called.
_____

7 He spoke with the need to eat well and exercise.
_____

8 Did you look the museum around?
_____

7 Put the words in the correct order to make sentences.

1 on / She / earrings / put / favourite / her
_____ .

2 TV / turned / on / I / the
_____ .

3 along / flatmate / get / new / I / my / with
_____ .

4 too / He / easily / up / gave
_____ .

5 while / I / out / with / my / brother / was / he / studied / hanging
_____ .

6 looking / car / She / was / new / buying / into / a
_____ .

7 I / out / yesterday / worked
_____ .

8 to / Remember / rubbish / the / out / take
_____ .

9 Tell / it / take / to / off / him
_____ .

8 Listen and choose the correct response. 🎧 31

1 **a** Yes, I wrote down his number.
 b Yes, I wrote his down number.

2 **a** We looked around the Opera House.
 b We looked the Opera House around.

3 **a** He grew with in New York.
 b He grew up in New York.

4 **a** Yes, I need to lie down and rest.
 b Yes, I need to lie off and rest.

5 **a** She woke at 7:30 up.
 b She woke up at 7:30.

6 **a** Let's eat out at the new Italian restaurant.
 b Let's eat about at the new Italian restaurant.

7 **a** Yes, I filled in all the information.
 b Yes, I filled all in the information.

8 **a** Sure. I'll turn it down now.
 b Sure. I'll turn down it now.

3D The amazing story of the man who gave us modern pain relief

TEDTALKS

AUTHENTIC LISTENING SKILLS

1 Listen to the TED Talk extracts and take notes. Choose the correct options to complete the sentences. 🎧 **32**

1 The *lion tamer* / *wire-walker* had an emergency during an act.

2 John J. Bonica didn't tell anyone that he *was a medical student* / *worked for the army*.

3 John spoke to *patients* / *doctors* to do research on pain.

4 John read *7,700* / *14,000* pages of medical textbooks. He found that the word *pain* appeared on *17.5* / *27* pages.

5 John wanted doctors to *understand pain* / *be more careful with surgeries*.

6 Hundreds of *pain clinics* / *hospitals* opened because of John's work.

WATCH ▶

2 Watch the TED Talk and put the events in the correct order.

_____ John writes the 'Bible of Pain.'

_____ The circus arrives in Brookfield, New York.

_____ John goes to Madigan Army Medical Center.

_____ There is an announcement that a doctor is needed.

_____ John gives the lion tamer mouth-to-mouth.

_____ John speaks to specialists and reads every medical textbook he can.

3 Underline the things that are true about John J. Bonica.

He used other names like Masked Marvel and Bull Walker.

He was a lion tamer.

He worked at a circus.

He was a nurse.

He had two jobs while he was in the circus.

He wrote a book about the circus.

He wanted to help patients feel better.

4 Complete each sentence about the talk with a word or short phrase.

1 The strongman _____ the lion tamer's life.

2 The strongman kept _____ from the other people to protect himself.

3 The same year, he was crowned the Light Heavyweight Champion _____.

4 Over the years, John had two jobs. He was a wrestler and _____.

5 John was _____ of all pain control in one of the largest army hospitals in America.

6 _____ had ever focused on pain like John had.

7 For the next _____ John would talk about pain.

8 The _____ wasn't to make patients better; it was to make patients to feel better.

VOCABULARY IN CONTEXT

5 Choose the correct meaning of the words in bold.

1 Alison **passed out** and fell to the ground after running ten miles.
   a stopped being awake
   b kept going
   c felt well

2 Mr Chen is **a specialist** who takes care of people with cancer.
   a a teacher
   b an expert
   c a writer

3 Louisa has three tests tomorrow, so she has to **hit the books** tonight.
   a borrow books from the library
   b study
   c hit books so they get softer

4 Edwin wants to create **an institution** that helps people with their pain.
   a an organization
   b a company
   c a website

5 My mum and dad **take** lies **seriously**. They don't get as angry about other things, but lying is not OK.
   a see as important
   b understand
   c don't know how to joke

6 Jisuk could not **ignore** the pain of others. She decided to become a doctor.
   a see
   b not think about
   c look at carefully

6 Bonica's contributions to science have helped millions of people live more comfortable lives. Can you give an example of someone in your life who has benefited from his work?

3E Opinions about health and happiness

SPEAKING

1 Put the phrases in the correct category. Then listen and check your answers. 🎧 33

Are you kidding?	Could you explain that a bit more?
I believe…	
I don't agree	I think…
I'm not sure about that.	In my opinion…
Really?	Sorry, but I don't think so.
Well, that's true…	Why do you say that?
You're right that…	

Saying what you think	Disagreeing
Asking follow-up questions	**Conceding a point**

2 Use the phrases from Exercise 1 to complete this conversation between two friends.

A It's so depressing, there are so many people getting ill these days because they don't do enough exercise.

B I know. And they say that getting more exercise actually makes you happier.

A **(1)** _____ everyone should have to do two hours of exercise every week. It should be the law.

B **(2)** _____. I think that's a bit extreme.

A **(3)** _____. The health system spends lots of money treating illnesses, when people could stop some problems by doing regular exercise.

B **(4)** _____. My grandad's 85 and since he's been swimming every day, he's been a lot healthier than my other grandparents. But **(5)** _____, you can't make people do exercise.

A **(6)** _____.

B Well, **(7)** _____ exercise is good for us, but it's not that simple. The reason some people may not enjoy exercise is that it actually causes them pain, and anyway, not everyone has enough time to exercise. Some people have really busy lives and have a family to take care of.

A **(8)** _____. Exercise reduces the risk of lots of diseases and lowers stress so
 (9) _____ people should make time to do this. It's their responsibility to stay healthy.

B **(10)** _____. I think it's each person's choice if they want to do exercise. There are other ways to stay healthy.

A **(11)** _____.

B Well, people can eat healthy food and not smoke or drink alcohol. Some people also take vitamins and do meditation, things like that.

A **(12)** _____. These things may help a little, but it's not the same as doing exercise to keep your body fit and working.

B Maybe, but I don't think you can make a law telling people they have to exercise.

3 Match the statements with their replies.

1 Teenagers are under more and more pressure from their friends these days. _____

2 Students have too much stress from school. _____

3 If you get ill in the jungle, you're going to die. _____

4 It would be great not to feel any pain. _____

5 Teenagers don't have very healthy diets. _____

6 The way to stay thin is to eat less. _____

7 Smartphones are really bad for your health. _____

8 I believe the best way to stay healthy is to exercise every day. _____

a **Are you kidding?** That's what stops us from getting more serious injuries.

b **I don't agree.** Your body needs a good supply of healthy food and some regular exercise.

c **I'm not sure about that.** Emergency health services can help you in most places.

d **In my opinion,** junk food should be banned from school canteens.

e **Really?** I think being happy is just as important for your health as exercise.

f **Sorry, but I don't think so.** People just worry about the effects of new technology.

g **Well, that's true.** Students don't have enough time to relax these days.

h **Yes, I think** social media makes the problem worse.

4 Listen and follow the instructions. You will hear three questions. Listen to each question and make notes about how you would answer it. Speak for at least one minute and record yourself. 🎧 34

5 Now listen to the model answers and compare them with your ideas. 🎧 35

WRITING An opinion essay

6 Put the words in the correct order to make sentences.

1 fast food / I think / convenient / While it's / that / is unhealthy, / true / very / it's

_____

_____ .

2 easier / believe that / understand / should / to / I / food labels / be

_____

_____ .

3 healthcare / opinion, / smokers / my / In / should / get / any / not

_____

_____ .

4 acceptable / sometimes / food / For / is / junk / me,

_____

_____ .

5 think this / us / I / reason / jealous / is / makes / that / feel / One / social media

_____

_____ .

6 because / don't / too / exercise / expensive / We / gym membership / is

_____

_____ .

7 right, / you're / but / Yes, / people / can't / some / exercise

_____

_____ .

7 Choose the correct options to complete the opinion essay.

> **Agree or disagree: Everyone should be forced to do one gym class every day**
>
> *One reason I think this is / While it's true that* joining gym classes is a good way to get exercise and stay healthy, *I think / because* forcing people to do it is a bad idea.
>
> *For me, / One reason I think this* is that we are less likely to do things we don't enjoy. So it's a bad idea *because / in my opinion* people stop enjoying anything they are forced to do. *I believe / For me,* that everyone should be encouraged to go to the gym, but not forced. Whatever people do to stay healthy should be their own choice.
>
> Secondly, *because / in my opinion*, many of us already exercise and stay healthy without going to the gym. For example, some people walk or cycle to school or work.
>
> *While it's true that / For me*, hiking in the countryside or swimming is how I get exercise. It's healthy… and it's fun!
>
> It doesn't matter how people exercise as long as they try to do some physical activity most days. Forcing everyone to go to daily gym classes will not work.

8 Read the opinion essay in Exercise 7 again. Are the statements true (T), false (F) or is the information not given (NG)?

1 The writer mainly disagrees with the statement. _____

2 The writer doesn't feel that getting exercise is important. _____

3 The writer thinks people should enjoy getting exercise. _____

4 The writer believes the gym is the best place to get exercise. _____

5 The writer exercises and is overweight. _____

6 Overall, the writer feels it's best if people have a choice. _____

9 In this writing exercise you will read a statement and write a response to it. In your written response, give your opinion with reasons and examples to support it.

We would be healthier if we stopped eating meat.

> To support your answer, use specific reasons and the expressions you have learned in this unit.

> **Acknowledging other ideas:**
> *While it's true that…, I think…*
>
> **Giving your opinion:**
> *I believe…*
> *In my opinion,…*
> *For me, …*
>
> **Giving reasons for your opinion:**
> *One reason I think this is…*
> *…because…*

Review

1 Choose the word that doesn't belong with the others.

1 mouth	ear	nose	knee
2 throat	elbow	hand	finger
3 stomachache	seasickness	happiness	high temperature
4 well	unwell	healthy	fine
5 doctor	virus	dentist	patient
6 feet	chest	arm	glasses
7 brain	lungs	chin	heart
8 medicine	illness	injury	pain

2 Read the descriptions of some parts of the body. What is the word for each one? The first letter is given for you.

1 It's the part of your leg that bends. k ___ ___ ___

2 It's the part of your arm that bends. e ___ ___ ___ ___

3 Dogs and cats have four of these, but birds and people have only two. l ___ ___ ___

4 Your toes are part of these. f ___ ___ ___

5 You have ten of these on your hands.
f ___ ___ ___ ___ ___ ___

6 You can hurt this if you fall or if you lift something very heavy. b ___ ___ ___

7 These are at the top of your arms, on either side of your neck. s ___ ___ ___ ___ ___ ___ ___ ___

8 It's where your food goes. s ___ ___ ___ ___ ___ ___

3 Complete the text with the correct quantifiers. There may be more than one correct answer.

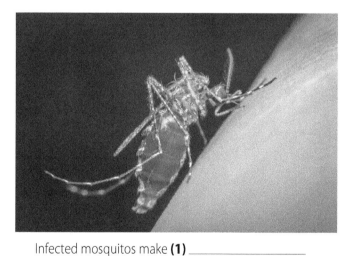

Infected mosquitos make **(1)** _____ people ill with malaria. **(2)** _____ people get ill from malaria? In 2015, about 210 million people in 91 countries had malaria and 400,000 people with malaria died. **(3)** _____ of the symptoms of malaria are fever, joint pain and headaches.

To protect against malaria, **(4)** _____ people hang mosquito nets over their beds. This keeps **(5)** _____ of the mosquitos away. Since 2000, UNICEF (United Nations International Children's Emergency Fund) has given out almost 1 billion nets in **(6)** _____ countries.

With medicine, **(7)** _____ people with malaria can get better. Organizations like Médecins Sans Frontières (Doctors Without Borders) provide treatment to **(8)** _____ people with malaria. In 2015, Médecins Sans Frontières treated 2.2 million cases of malaria.

4 Complete the sentences with the correct quantifier and phrasal verb. In some sentences there may be more than one correct answer.

bring back	hand in	pick up	put on
sit down	spoke about	wrote down	

1 I _____ _____ notes during the lesson.

2 _____ essays did you _____ last week?

3 Do you want to _____ _____ music _____?

4 Did you _____ _____ dinner _____ with you?

5 _____ food did you _____ on your way home?

6 _____ people at the meeting _____ the need for a new gym.

7 _____ times a day do you _____ to check your email?

5 Circle the phrasal verb which can **not** be separated.

1 *look around / call back / keep up*

2 *write down / speak about / take off*

3 *turn down / look after / take up*

4 *deal with / fill in / pass on*

5 *put on / bring back / complain of*

6 *grow up / write down / hand in*

❹ Learning

4A How we learn

VOCABULARY Education

① Revision Label the photos with the correct words.

classroom	dictionary	homework	library
map	teacher	university	

1 _____

2 _____

3 _____

4 _____

5 _____

6 _____

7 _____

② Revision Choose the correct words to complete the sentences.

1 My favourite *class / classroom* is Spanish. Today's *lesson / teach* was about the past tense.

2 When I don't understand a word, I look it up in my English-Spanish *map / dictionary*.

3 I always *teach / pass* all of my exams. I work hard because I don't want to *fail / take*.

4 My classes start at 7:30am. I have to take the *books / school bus* at 7:00. Sometimes it's late, but usually I am the one who is late!

5 My classes end at 2:15pm, but in the evening I have a lot of *maps / homework* to do.

6 There are a lot of books in our school *library / university*.

7 My mother *fails / teaches* Chinese classes at the *dictionary / university*.

③ Fill in the missing vowels to form more words about school.

1 b __ cr __ __ t __ v __

2 h __ rd-w __ rk __ ng

3 pr __ m __ ry sch __ __ l

4 n __ t __ b __ __ k

5 d __ v __ l __ p sk __ lls

6 __ n __ d __ c __ t __ __ n

7 __ nl __ n __ l __ __ rn __ ng

8 g __ __ d gr __ d __ s

9 t __ k __ __ x __ ms

④ Match the words or phrases with the definitions.

1 what students write in
2 to go to classes
3 to become good at something
4 to have new, interesting ideas
5 to do and study a lot
6 piece of furniture students sit at
7 learning
8 internet-based classes
9 what you get in a class to show how you did

a desk
b be creative
c notebook
d online learning
e attend school
f be hard-working
g develop a skill
h grade
i education

⑤ Complete the sentences with the correct words.

1 It's important to get an e_____. At school, children learn and develop s_____ they will need in life, like reading and maths.

2 In developed countries, most children a_____ school during the day. Younger children go to p_____ school, and older children go to s_____ school.

3 In a typical classroom, students sit at d_____ and the teacher stands in front and writes on a b_____.

4 The government pays for s_____ schools, so all children can go there. Some parents choose to pay to send their children to p_____ schools. These can be very expensive.

5 Class s_____ can vary a lot. There may be only three or four students in a class, or there may be 30–40! It depends on the area and the school.

6 School is usually fun for younger students, but as they get older, it gets more difficult. They start to worry about taking t_____ and getting good g_____.

6 Complete the text with the correct words.

attend	classes	creative	desks
develop	education (x2)	free	online learning
primary	students	study	teacher

In rural Bangladesh, heavy rains make it hard for many children to **(1)** _____ school. An organization called Shidhulai Swanirvar Sangstha found a **(2)** _____ solution to this problem: Floating **(3)** _____ schools! Twenty boats pick up children near their homes, then they stop and **(4)** _____ begin. So the boats are both school buses *and* classrooms! Inside, there are **(5)** _____ and chairs for the **(6)** _____, and a board for the **(7)** _____ to write on. There are also computers with internet for **(8)** _____.
The children **(9)** _____ for three hours on the boats, then they go home and work on their homework.
Some of their parents go to the floating schools, too. There are seven boats for adult **(10)** _____.
In the classrooms, the men and women **(11)** _____ skills for farming and good health. The schools for both the children and the adults are **(12)** _____ so they don't have to pay for their **(13)** _____.

Learning **39**

7 **Extension** Write the subjects in the correct category.

algebra	biology	chemistry	drama club
geography	geometry	history	orchestra
physics	sports		

Science: _____

_____

Maths: _____

_____

Social sciences: _____

_____

After-school activities: _____

_____

_____

8 **Extension** Write the class or club that each person belongs in.

algebra	ancient history	band	biology
chemistry	drama club	social sciences	sports team

1 I'm interested in plants and animals.

_____

2 I like reading about people who lived a very long time ago. _____

3 I play football and tennis. _____

4 I want to be a theatre actor or maybe be in films. _____

5 I'm learning to play the guitar. I love pop and rock music. _____

6 I want to learn about other cultures and the world we live in. _____

7 I enjoy finding out what things are made of. I also like doing interesting experiments! _____

8 I'm good with numbers, but I'd like to develop my skills more. _____

9 I play the violin. I love Mozart and Beethoven.

_____

PRONUNCIATION Linking and elision

9 Listen and underline the stressed word. 🎧 36

1 Saruka is hopeful about attending college in Kyoto next year.
2 The test was stressful because I didn't revise for it.
3 Alex was thankful his teacher allowed extra time to complete the homework.
4 Haru didn't get a good grade on the maths test because he made careless mistakes.
5 Maria thinks computers are a useful way to learn.

LISTENING

10 Listen and choose the subject that each speaker talks about. 🎧 37

1 **a** history
  b geography
  c art

2 **a** computing
  b art history
  c a foreign language

3 **a** science
  b geography
  c history

4 **a** maths
  b physical education
  c science

5 **a** maths
  b computing
  c a foreign language

6 **a** music
  b physical education
  c maths

11 Listen and choose the best title for the talk. 🎧 38

a Remote education
b Online classes
c Distance learning
d Modern technology

12 Listen to the speaker again and answer the questions. 🎧 38

1 How many other names does the speaker use for distance learning?
  a one
  b two
  c three

2 What does the speaker say makes online learning possible?
  a the internet and computers
  b colleges and universities
  c teachers and students

3 What adjective does the speaker use for areas that are distant and isolated?
  a faraway
  b remote
  c secluded

4 What does the *e* in *e-learning* stand for?
  a everybody
  b electronic
  c everything

5 What is one reason the speaker gives for people not choosing e-learning?
  a wanting to be with other students
  b fear of being with others
  c frustration with technology

6 What is another word for *choices* that the author uses?
  a opinions
  b opportunities
  c options

13 Listen and complete the sentences. 🎧 39

1 Online learning is a lot _____ for me than attending a college.
2 Technology is _____ for me. I prefer to be in a classroom.
3 My online classes are _____ expensive than attending a university.
4 Learning with others is _____ interesting than studying alone.
5 I think distance education is clearly the _____ way to learn.
6 I'm happy that people have lots of _____ these days.

GRAMMAR Comparatives and superlatives

14 Complete the sentences with the comparative form of the adjective in brackets.

1 I want to buy a _____ (big) desk, so I can see my notes and my books at the same time.
2 My new chair is _____ (comfortable) than the one I used to have in my bedroom.
3 My eyes don't hurt now when I read because I'm using a _____ (bright) lamp.
4 I can use several programs at the same time on that _____ (good) computer.
5 This year, our teacher chose _____ (interesting) books, so our classes are more fun.
6 I need a _____ (large) notebook because this one is almost full!
7 I'm going to ask my friends to recommend some _____ (cool) music to listen to when I study. My music is quite boring.
8 I asked for a _____ (expensive) laptop because I need more storage space.

15 Complete the sentences with the correct comparative form of the adverbs.

attentively	clearly	early	fast
hard	often	regularly	well

1 How should I change my study habits to do _____ in school?
2 I need to work _____ so I can get better grades.
3 When I do my homework _____, I don't need to work so much before tests.
4 I could ask the teacher to explain things I don't understand if I read the textbook _____.
5 I know I need to listen to my teachers _____.
6 I should write _____ so I can read my notes and study from them later.
7 The students who started revising for the test _____ got a better grade than me.
8 I need to write much _____ in exams so I have enough time to answer all the questions.

16 Put the words in the correct order to make sentences.

1 the best / in the whole city / is / school / Our school
_____ .
2 nicer / and bigger / the other schools / than / near here / is / The building
_____ .
3 than / are / better / teachers in / other schools / Our teachers
_____ .

4 place / in the school / The library / the quietest / is
_____ .
5 has / computers / Our / computer lab / the fastest
_____ .
6 the other / than / classes / is / My class / better
_____ .
7 because we / learning / We work / than / harder / like / other classes
_____ .
8 also have / football team / We / best / the
_____ .
9 class / other classes / My / higher / than / grades / gets
_____ .

17 Write questions using the correct superlative form of the words in bold.

1 **A** what / **old** / university in the world?
_____
   B The University of Karueein (also known as Al Quaraouiyine University) in Morocco started in 859.
2 **A** what country / **large** / number of students?
_____
   B According to the 2011 census, there are 315 million students in India, which has a population of 1.3 billion people.
3 **A** where / **big** / school in the world?
_____
   B In India. The Lucknow City Montessori School in Uttar Pradesh has 2,500 teachers who teach more than 52,000 students in 1,000 classrooms.
4 **A** how big / **small** / school in the world?
_____
   B A school in Turin, Italy, has just one student.
5 **A** who / **old** / high-school graduate in the US?
_____
   B Fred Butler was 106 years old when he graduated from high school.
6 **A** who / **young** / high-school graduate in the US?
_____
   B Michael Kearney graduated from high school when he was six years old! He graduated from university when he was eight!
7 **A** where / students / **long** and **short** / summer holidays?
_____
   B In Ethiopia, some schools have twelve to fifteen weeks of summer holidays. In Germany, most students have only six weeks of summer holidays.
8 **A** where / students / receive / **more** / homework?
_____
   B In China, where students have to do more than fourteen hours of homework a week!

4B Outdoor classroom

VOCABULARY BUILDING Suffixes *-ful/-less*

1 Complete the sentences with the correct form of the word in brackets. Add the suffix *-ful* or *-less* and make changes to spelling where necessary.

1 Finnish schools believe that studying subjects together is more _____ (use) than studying them separately.

2 When students work together, they may be more _____ (care) about what they do than when they work alone.

3 Learning about _____ (beauty) works of art is part of a complete education.

4 Working together in groups can help students become more _____ (skill) learners.

5 Working with a group is a good way to avoid making _____ (care) mistakes.

6 Students should be more _____ (thank) for the help that teachers give them.

READING

2 Read the text and choose the correct options.

1 According to paragraph 1, which of the following is true of Finnish schools?
   a Students only learn about their favourite subjects.
   b Finnish schools don't teach history and geography.
   c Students learn about different subjects at the same time.
   d Students work in cafés.

2 Which TWO of these points about Finnish schools does the writer make?
   a Working in groups is a good way to become good communicators.
   b Some students prefer to study science rather than geography or history.
   c Studying topics, as opposed to subjects, is a useful way to learn.
   d Finnish students study maths, art and history.

3 According to paragraph 3, how is Finland making changes to learning environments?
   a by creating courses about World War II
   b by encouraging students to work in groups
   c by building new school buildings without separate classrooms or hallways
   d by preparing students for jobs in the future

4 According to the article, what do students learn by studying topics instead of subjects?
   a They learn how to look for a job.
   b They study the history of wars, including World Wars I and II.
   c They develop the skills needed to work in a restaurant.
   d They learn to share information and apply skills to a variety of tasks.

5 In the article as a whole, the writer appears to feel that
   a schools should have separate classrooms and hallways.
   b recent changes in Finnish education are good for students.
   c some students prefer to work alone and not in groups.
   d most Finnish teachers usually work very long days.

3 Choose the correct option (a–d) to complete each sentence.

1 According to the article, _____ subjects together.
2 Rather than study subjects on their own, _____ way to learn.
3 Working in groups, _____ work together successfully.
4 Studying one subject at a time _____ them together.

   a working together is the best
   b isn't as useful as studying
   c students in Finland study some
   d students need to be able to

4 Match the headings with the paragraphs in the article.

   a The advantages of working together
   b The new approach in practice
   c Finland's new approach to education
   d Giving students the skills to succeed

Paragraph 1 _____
Paragraph 2 _____
Paragraph 3 _____
Paragraph 4 _____

What do you want to know?

1 🎧 **40** What's your favourite school subject? Do you love maths? Does English interest you? Are you not as excited about art as you are about music? Or are you more of a science buff*? We all have favourite subjects, but what if, instead of learning about each subject separately, you studied two or more together? That's exactly how some students in Finland are learning.

2 When students learn about topics such as world events, they study several subjects together. For example, in a course about World War II, the students study history, geography and maths. Learning about topics, not just one subject, helps students see several points of view. In another course*, called 'Working in a café,' students study English language, communication skills and economics. In courses like this, students use many skills as they are learning.

3 Finnish educators* believe that students learn better when they work in small groups to solve problems.

Working together is a very useful skill that helps students develop their ability to communicate. At this point, students in Finland don't spend their whole school day working in groups. They still attend 'regular' classes and study some subjects separately. But Finland is serious about making changes to the school day and to how students learn. The country has already built several new school buildings that don't have separate classrooms or hallways.

4 Finnish schools are making this change because many educators there believe that working together to study topics is the best way to learn. They believe that working alone and studying only one subject at a time isn't the best way to learn. They feel that students who work together with teachers and other students to choose and study topics they care about are better learners. They also feel that students who learn in this way are better prepared for jobs, once they've completed their education.

buff *a fan; someone who likes something a lot*
course *class*

educators *teachers and school directors*

4C Skills for life

GRAMMAR Comparative forms

1 Complete the sentences with *so* or *such*.

1 Computer skills are _____ important for students.
2 There is _____ a need for computers in every classroom.
3 The book was _____ interesting Airi read it in one day!
4 Tomas is _____ a talented writer. Do you read his blog?
5 That test was _____ easy!
6 The English exam was _____ challenging.
7 We saw _____ a fun play on Friday night.
8 My nephew and niece both got top grades; they are _____ clever children.

2 Listen and complete the sentences. 🎧 41

1 Victor hopes the essay he wrote is _____. It's 200 words.
2 Grammar is _____ vocabulary for me.
3 Studying for your exams is _____ doing your homework.
4 I thought our homework was _____.
5 The classroom wasn't _____ for fourteen students.
6 My classmate decided the study group wasn't _____ for her to attend.
7 Watching films in English is _____!
8 I watched _____ film last weekend.

3 Choose the correct option to complete the sentences.

1 Playing football **isn't as fun as** swimming.
   The phrase *isn't as… as …* _____.
   a shows that the quality described by an adjective is more than wanted or needed
   b compares things and says how they are similar or different
   c makes the adjective stronger

2 My soup was **not hot enough**, so I sent it back.
   The phrase *not… enough* _____.
   a shows that the quality described by an adjective is more than wanted or needed
   b says that the quality described by the adjective is the right amount
   c says that the quality described by the adjective is less than the right amount

3 Tom has **such a great** car.
   The word *such* _____.
   a shows that the quality described by an adjective is more than wanted or needed
   b compares things and says how they are similar or different
   c makes the adjective stronger

4 His score was **high enough** to earn him an award.
   The word *enough* _____.
   a shows that the quality described by an adjective is more than wanted or needed
   b says that the quality described by the adjective is the right amount
   c says that the quality described by the adjective is less than the right amount

5 I love that book! It's **so interesting**.
   The word *so* _____.
   a shows that the quality described by an adjective is more than wanted or needed
   b compares things and says how they are similar or different
   c makes the adjective stronger

6 This shirt is **too big** for me.
   The word *too* _____.
   a shows that the quality described by an adjective is more than wanted or needed
   b compares things and says how they are similar or different
   c makes the adjective stronger

4 Are the words in bold correct or incorrect? Correct those that are incorrect.

1 It is **such cold** today. _____
2 Chen isn't **as old enough** his brother. _____
3 The wifi in this café is **so bad**. _____
4 The train is **enough fast** to get us to Granada by 4:00. _____
5 This is **such a slow bus**. I don't think we'll get to class on time. _____
6 The bus was **enough slow** – we didn't get to class on time. _____
7 Is it **hot such** to go swimming today? _____
8 My maths class has three students in it. It **isn't as big as** my English class. _____
9 Alex is **so a bad** loser – he gets really angry if he doesn't win. _____

5 Choose the option which is closer in meaning to the original sentence.

1 Maths is as easy as history.
   a Maths is easy and history is easy.
   b History is not as challenging as maths.

2 My new neighbourhood is a lot safer than where I lived last year.
   a My old neighbourhood isn't as safe as my new neighbourhood.
   b My new neighbourhood isn't as safe as my old neighbourhood.

3 Lara's car wasn't big enough for us all to travel in.
   a Lara's car was small enough.
   b Lara's car was too small.

4 Antoni's car is noisy. Lila's car is quiet.
   a Antoni's car isn't as quiet as Lila's car.
   b Lila's car isn't as quiet as Antoni's car.

5 I went to Athens, but I was only there for two days. It was a very quick trip!
   a My trip to Athens was quick enough.
   b My trip to Athens was so quick.

6 Katya thinks studying is as important as working to make money.
   a Katya thinks studying is important enough.
   b Katya thinks studying is important. She also thinks making money is important.

7 I wasn't old enough to see that film.
   a I was too young to see that film.
   b I was so young to see that film.

8 It is very challenging to climb Mt. Everest.
   a Mt. Everest is such a challenging mountain to climb.
   b Mt. Everest is challenging enough to climb.

6 Complete the second sentence so that it means the same as the first. Use no more than three words in each gap.

1 I thought the exam was very stressful.
   I thought the exam was _____ stressful.

2 That coffee was awful!
   That was _____ bad coffee.

3 I am seventeen years old and my friend Zach is seventeen years old.
   I am _____ Zach.

4 Wei is very popular, but his friend Kwan is not.
   Kwan _____ as Wei.

5 I really loved that book!
   That book was _____ good!

6 I needed to get to the theatre by 8:00 to get a good seat; I got there at 7:50.
   I got to the theatre early _____.

7 I gave up because I was afraid.
   I gave up because I wasn't _____.

7 Put the words in the correct order to make sentences.

1 was / cool / The / to / drink / enough / tea
   _____.

2 The / too / were / hot / peppers
   _____.

3 We / enough / to / have / a / salad / vegetables / make
   _____.

4 There / people / were / to / class / play / the / game / in / enough
   _____.

5 My / tomorrow / is / at / the / important / school / interview / so
   _____.

6 teacher / us / Our / easy / gave / an / such / test
   _____.

7 as / Josh / father / is / as / his / tall
   _____.

8 can / as / I / run / as / can / fast / Leo
   _____.

8 Choose the correct option to complete the sentences.

1 My tea was too hot, so
   a I didn't drink it.
   b I heated it up.

2 The birthday cake was so good, that
   a I didn't have any.
   b I ate two pieces.

3 He wasn't serious enough when he practised for the competition, so
   a he came in last place.
   b he came in first place.

4 The chemistry course wasn't challenging enough for me, so
   a I took a different class.
   b I got a bad grade.

5 She doesn't think watching TV is as interesting as seeing films, so
   a she went to see a film.
   b she stayed home and watched TV.

6 I had enough money to buy my mum a really nice birthday present, so
   a my mum was sad and didn't like her present.
   b my mum loved her present and was really happy.

7 The trip took such a long time, so
   a we got there late at night and were really tired.
   b we got there really quickly and had a lot of time to relax before bed.

4D Don't eat the marshmallow!

TEDTALKS

AUTHENTIC LISTENING SKILLS

1 Listen to the TED Talk extracts. Choose the correct option to complete the sentences. 🎧 **42**

1 In the US research, *one out of three / two out of three* children ate the marshmallow.

2 *One out of three / Two out of three* children did other things, like walking around.

3 *A great percentage / A few* of the children who ate the marshmallows were in trouble years later.

4 In Colombia, *one out of three / two out of three* ate the marshmallow.

5 Joachim made *one / two* marshmallow book(s) for children in Korea.

WATCH ▷

2 Watch the TED Talk and choose the correct answers.

1 Who started the first research?
   a Joachim de Posada
   b a group of children
   c a professor at Stanford

2 How long did the children have to wait in the room?
   a four minutes
   b fifteen minutes
   c two hours

3 What did the children get if they waited?
   a one more marshmallow
   b two more marshmallows
   c coffee

4 What does Joachim de Posada say is the most important factor for success?
   a being able to control yourself
   b knowing how to get more of what you want
   c asking for a better opportunity or deal

5 What did Joachim want to find out in Colombia?
   a if Hispanic children liked marshmallows
   b if Hispanic children acted differently to American children
   c if the first research was correct

6 Why does Joachim think the research is so important?
   a People are eating too many sweets like marshmallows.
   b People should teach their children to stop eating sweets.
   c People are using more than they are giving back.

3 Match the words with the correct paraphrased line.

1 principle   a I'm here because I have **something very important to say**.

2 question   b I think we have found the most important **reason** for success.

3 experiment c The children already, at four, understood the most important **rule** for success.

4 message   d I have **something I want to ask**…

5 factor   e I did the same **test** in Colombia.

4 Underline the things that are true about the children who did not eat the marshmallows.

They knew how to wait.

They grew up to be successful.

They did not like marshmallows.

They did not make it to university.

They had good grades.

They were in trouble.

They had good eating habits.

They were happy.

VOCABULARY IN CONTEXT

5 Listen and complete each sentence with the correct word or short phrase. 🎧 **43**

1 What did they find? They went to look for these kids who were now eighteen and nineteen. And they found that _____ of the children that had not eaten the marshmallow were successful.

2 A great percentage of the kids that ate the marshmallow, they _____.

3 They did not _____ university. They had bad grades. Some of them dropped out.

4 This little girl was interesting; she ate the inside of the marshmallow. _____, she wanted us to think that she had not eaten it, so she would get two. But she ate it.

5 She should not _____ banking, for example, or work at a cash register. But she will be successful.

6 We are eating more marshmallows than we are _____. Thank you so much.

4E Such a cool subject!

SPEAKING

1 Read the conversation and complete the sentences with the correct phrases. Then listen to the conversation and check your answers. 🎧 44

is the best choice	isn't as useful as this
isn't it expensive	look the most useful
looks more exciting	more interesting
think it's useful enough (x2)	too boring

A Hey, I'm looking for an app to practise my English with, do you know any?

B Ah, that's a good idea. I've never thought of that. Which ones **(1)** _____?

A Well, there's this one here, which has flash cards and some grammar exercises, and it's free.

B Is it **(2)** _____, maybe?

A I don't know, it's for school anyway, but do you **(3)** _____?

B Well, you get what you pay for. What about that one, with the star logo?

A That looks **(4)** _____. There are things to read and listen to.

B And there are some collocation activities for vocabulary too.

A Excellent! Teachers always tell us to practise them. We'll be awesome.

B Yeah, that first one **(5)** _____.

A Are there any more?

B I had a look and there's this one. It **(6)** _____, with lots of games to play with words and grammar.

A Let's see. Oh, yeah, but **(7)** _____?

B Well, it is a little. Do you **(8)** _____ to pay for?

A I'm not sure. I guess you have to pay to find out.

B Yeah. I think the star one **(9)** _____.

2 You're writing an article for the school website about things students like and dislike about the school.

Think about the three different people described below and make notes about what their answers to the questions might be. Then listen to the model answers to compare your ideas. 🎧 45

- A student in the first year at the school, who is quite lazy.
- A student in their last year at school, who is captain of the football team.
- A student in the middle of school, who plans to go to university.

1 What's the most fun thing about being at this school?
2 Which subjects are the most interesting?
3 Do you think that school is useful enough for your future?

3 Listen and follow the instructions. 🎧 46

Listen to the model answer and compare it with your ideas. 🎧 47

WRITING An enquiry email

4 Choose the correct answers to the questions.

1 What greeting would you use in an email to someone you don't know?
  a Dear Evening Class Coordinator,
  b Hi Evening Class Coordinator,

2 How would you say how you know about the course?
  a I'm really interested in this course.
  b I saw an advertisement for this course online.

3 How would you introduce your reason for emailing?
  a I wanted to do a course in printmaking last year.
  b I'm writing because I have a couple of questions.

4 What kind of information would you ask?
  a Are all the materials for the course provided?
  b Do you prefer printmaking or photography?

5 How would you thank the person you are emailing?
  a Thank you in advance for any information.
  b Thanks a lot. I really appreciate your help!

6 What closing expression would you use?
  a See you soon,
  b Yours sincerely,

5 Put the six sections of the enquiry email in the correct order.

_____ First, is the course suitable for complete beginners? Second, is there a focus on sound editing or do you mainly cover mixing techniques?
_____ Dario Cafolla
_____ Thanks for any information you can provide. I look forward to hearing from you.
_____ Yours sincerely,
_____ I saw your poster for the five-day music production course when I was at the train station this morning. I'm writing because I'd like some more information.
_____ Dear Sound Studios,

6 Read the enquiry email. Then choose the correct information for the categories. There are two items you don't need.

> Dear Sound Studios,
>
> I saw your poster for the five-day music production course when I was at the train station this morning. I'm writing because I'd like some more information.
>
> First, is the course suitable for complete beginners? Second, is there a focus on sound editing or do you mainly cover mixing techniques?
>
> Thanks for any information you can provide. I look forward to hearing from you.
>
> Yours sincerely,
> Dario Cafolla

Dario Cafolla	five days	formal
informal	music production	sound editing
Sound Studios	train station	

1 Course venue: _____
2 Course title: _____
3 Length of course: _____
4 Question: _____
5 Sender: _____
6 Tone of email: _____

7 Read the enquiry email. Find and correct six mistakes in it.

> Dear Happy Language School,
>
> I saw you're advertisement for the four-week course in Business English on your website. I'd like to ask about a couple of things.
>
> First, what is the language level of most students who take this course? First, is your Certificate of Achievement recognized by industry professionals!
>
> Thanks for any informations you can give me. I look forward to hearing for you.
>
> Your sincerely,
> Joan Cho

8 This is part of an advertisement for a course you have seen online.

> **Introduction to lead guitar**
> Experienced instructor gives group lessons every Monday, 6pm to 8pm. Efficient teaching method. Useful exercises, techniques and tips. Contact *Guitar Experts Inc.* at info@ GEI.com.

Now, write an enquiry email to the course directors. Follow the instructions:

- say where you saw the course advertised and why you are emailing
- ask about the style of music taught and the cost of a lesson
- use polite language for your greeting, closing statement and closing expressions.

Review

1 Choose the correct options to complete the sentences.

1 Teachers give _____ to students to see what they have learned.
- **a** skills
- **b** tests
- **c** grades
- **d** notebooks

2 Teachers give _____ to show students how well they did in the class.
- **a** pens
- **b** education
- **c** grades
- **d** skills

3 For _____, you need a computer, tablet or smartphone.
- **a** classrooms
- **b** online learning
- **c** private school
- **d** studying maths

4 A hard-working student _____.
- **a** sometimes attends school
- **b** never does homework
- **c** gets bad grades
- **d** always revises for tests

2 Look at the scrambled words. Unscramble them and match them with the correct descriptions.

enolni rangilen	ypirmra closoh	ontobesko
sksde	estta loshosc	apiretv coolsh

1 Students sit at these when they study.

_____

2 Students write with pens in these.

_____

3 You need the internet for this. _____
4 They are free for all students. _____
5 Classes here are for very young students.

_____

6 You pay for your education here. _____

3 Complete the tables with the correct forms of the comparative and superlative adjectives and adverbs.

Adjective	Comparative	Superlative
bad	worse	
old	older	
useful	more useful	
big		the biggest
hard-working		the most hard-working
interesting		the most interesting

Adverb	Comparative	Superlative
fast		the fastest
late	later	
hard		the hardest
well	better	
recently	more recently	
slowly		the most slowly
quietly		the most quietly

4 Complete the conversation with the correct words.

best	better	important enough
is as important as	isn't as enjoyable as	more useful
so enjoyable	too hard	

A I think swimming is **(1)** _____.

B I think swimming **(2)** _____ playing football. Football is the **(3)** _____!

A I am **(4)** _____ at swimming than I am at playing football.

B I think sports are a fun way to stay healthy! But what do you think – is it **(5)** _____ to eat well or exercise a lot?

A Experts say eating well **(6)** _____ exercising.

B Yes, but sometimes it is **(7)** _____ to find enough time to exercise.

A I agree, but exercising is **(8)** _____ to make sure you do it every day.

5 Family and friends

5A The people in my life

VOCABULARY How's it going?

Darrell
Stephanie
Alana
Michael

1 Revision Look at the photo. Choose the correct words to complete the sentences.

1 They are *friends / a family*.
2 Michael is a *boy / man*.
3 Alana is a *girl / woman*.
4 Alana and Darrell are *married / divorced*.
5 Stephanie is Darrell's *son / daughter*.
6 Darrell is Michael's *father / mother*.
7 Alana and Darrell are Stephanie and Michael's *children / parents*.
8 Darrell is Alana's *wife / husband*.

2 Revision Complete the sentences with the correct words.

1 Before people get married, they are s __ __ __ __ __.
2 If a man was married, but now he's not, he's d __ v __ __ __ __ __.
3 Your mother and father are your p __ __ __ __ __ __.
4 Boys and girls are c __ __ l __ __ __ __.
5 Fathers are m __ __.
6 Mothers are w __ __ __ __.

3 Put the people into the correct category.

aunt	brother	classmate	cousin	daughter
father	friend	husband	mother	partner
sister	son	stranger	uncle	wife

man / boy	woman / girl	either

4 Match the words with the definitions.

1 aunt   **a** a person you don't know
2 uncle   **b** a person you play football or cricket with
3 partner   **c** touch someone's cheek with your lips
4 teammate   **d** the brother of your mother or father
5 stranger   **e** move your hand in the air
6 kiss   **f** put your arms around someone
7 hug   **g** a person you work together with on a project
8 wave   **h** the sister of your mother or father

5 Listen and match 1–6 with the photos. 🎧 48

a

b

c

d

e

f

1 _____
2 _____
3 _____
4 _____
5 _____
6 _____

6 Choose the correct words to complete the text.

A big family

Having a big family can be fun. I have one older **(1)** _____ and he's not always nice to me, but I also have three younger **(2)** _____ and we are very close. We live with our parents and my **(3)** _____, who is my father's mother. Her husband, my **(4)** _____, died two years ago.

My father was an only child, but my grandparents on my mother's side had two sons and four daughters, which means I have two **(5)** _____ and three **(6)** _____.They all had children, too, so I have a lot of **(7)** _____ on that side of the family.

There are also some other people I think of as part of my family, for example my **(8)** _____. She comes to my house every weekend and celebrates holidays with us, too. There are also my volleyball **(9)** _____. We are like a family at school; we're always together and helping each other.

1 a sister   **b** father   **c** brother   **d** stranger
2 a sisters   **b** parents   **c** aunts   **d** classmates
3 a aunt   **b** grandmother   **c** uncle   **d** grandfather
4 a aunt   **b** grandmother   **c** uncle   **d** grandfather
5 a mothers   **b** cousins   **c** aunts   **d** uncles
6 a brothers   **b** grandfathers   **c** aunts   **d** uncles
7 a partners   **b** cousins   **c** brothers and sisters   **d** strangers
8 a stranger   **b** friend of a friend   **c** best friend   **d** cousin
9 a classmates   **b** teammates   **c** strangers   **d** partners

7 Complete the sentences with the correct words and phrases.

best friend	classmate	neighbour	partner	say hello
shake	strangers	teammates	wave	

1 When I meet someone for the first time, I smile and _____ their hand.
2 When I see my friends across the street, I _____ my hand and _____.
3 In class, we often have to work with a _____ on an activity.
4 A lot of people don't enjoy talking to _____ on the bus or the train, but there are some people who are friendly with everyone!
5 Simon is my _____. He lives just across the street.

6 In a basketball game, all of the _____ must work together to win.
7 Some people don't have just one _____, but many different people who they spend a lot of time with.
8 I don't know Annabel very well, but she's a _____; we study French together.

8 Extension What is each person's relationship to Rachel, the second speaker? Listen and circle the answers.
🎧 **49**

1	Dan	brother	stepbrother
2	Steve	stepfather	father-in-law
3	Max	half-brother	stepbrother
4	April	sister-in-law	stepsister
5	Olivia	niece	half-sister
6	Amanda	sister-in-law	half-sister
7	Jared	half-brother	nephew

9 Extension Complete the text with the correct words.

brother-in-law	ex-wife	father-in-law
half-brother	half-sister	mother-in-law
nephews	nieces	stepbrothers
stepfather	stepmother	stepsisters

Our families often grow as we do. If you have a sister and she gets married, then you will have a new **(1)**_____. If they have children, you will have **(2)** _____ and **(3)** _____. Then, if you get married, you will have a husband or wife, and his or her mother and father will become your **(4)** _____ and **(5)** _____.

Or, you might become part of a blended family. When a married couple gets divorced, or someone loses a wife or husband, sometimes they get married again. The man marries a new woman and his children get a **(6)** _____. If his new wife has children, too, then his children will also have new **(7)** _____ and **(8)** _____. If the father and his new wife have a baby together, this child will be the **(9)** _____ or **(10)** _____ of the children from the first marriages. If the man's **(11)** _____ also marries someone new, then the kids will also have a **(12)** _____ and another new family!

PRONUNCIATION Past form endings

⑩ Read the sentences aloud and write the pronunciation of the *-ed* verb you hear. Write /d/, /t/, or /ɪd/. Then listen and check your answers. 🎧 50

1 I've already selected my outfit for the party. _____
2 I learned how to dance from my father. _____
3 Have you tasted the cake yet? _____
4 My uncle photographed the football team. _____
5 I tried to invite her, but she said no. _____
6 Everyone at the celebration looked great! _____
7 We haven't celebrated yet. _____
8 My aunt was ill so she stayed at home. _____

LISTENING

⑪ Listen to the conversations (1–6). Are the statements correct (YES) or incorrect (NO)? Tick the boxes. 🎧 51

	YES	NO
1 He invited her to the party.	☐	☐
2 She invited him to the celebration.	☐	☐
3 She accepted his invitation.	☐	☐
4 He didn't accept the invitation.	☐	☐
5 She accepted his invitation.	☐	☐
6 She invited everyone to the celebration.	☐	☐

⑫ Listen to the speaker and complete the text with the correct words. 🎧 52

I recently graduated from Manchester University. We had a fantastic **(1)** _____ with my family and friends. And, to be honest, it was both sad and happy for me. Sad because I'm leaving a lot of people that I've **(2)** _____ for years. Happy because a whole new period in my life is beginning and I feel really excited about what the future holds.

Fantastically, I've been **(3)** _____ two different jobs. I haven't decided which one to take **(4)** _____, but they're both good. I feel really lucky. And my parents are really supportive. They want me to follow my dreams. My mother told me that she'll be **(5)** _____ of me no matter what I decide to do.

It's impossible to predict the future, but I feel really good about things. I'm **(6)** _____, I have a wonderful family and I feel like almost anything is possible. I'd better stop talking before I get too **(7)** _____.

⑬ Listen to the sentences about each photo. Write the letter (a, b, c or d) of the sentence that best describes the photo. 🎧 53

1 _____

2 _____

3 _____

4 _____

GRAMMAR Present perfect and past simple

14 Choose the correct verb forms to complete the exchanges.

1 A How long *have / had / has* you had your computer?

B I haven't *has / had / having* it very long – only a year.

2 A How many books has Ms Brenner *ask / asks / asked* you to read this term?

B She *has / have / had* given us two books so far.

3 A *Had / Has / Have* you found your smartphone yet? I know you had it yesterday.

B No, I *don't have / haven't / haven't had*. I don't know where it is.

4 A Have you *knows / known / know* your best friend for a long time?

B Yes, I have. We *had / having / have* been friends since we were ten!

5 A How many years has our class *studies / study / studied* English? Three? Four?

B I think we have *has / have / had* English for four years now. We're getting pretty good!

6 A I have *work / worked / works* at the bookshop since the summer. I really like it.

B That's awesome! *Has / Had / Have* you thought about working there when you finish school?

15 Rewrite the negative sentences in the affirmative and the affirmative sentences in the negative.

Example: Marco hasn't finished his homework.
Marco has finished his homework.

1 Celia has seen her parents all day.
_____

2 Yuri and Natasha have seen a lot of really good films.
_____

3 Our teacher has given us a lot of homework this weekend.
_____

4 My friends have not called yet.
_____

5 I haven't met my best friend's sister.
_____

16 Complete the text with the present perfect form of the verbs in brackets.

My family and I like to travel. We **(1)** _____ (take) advantage of every chance to travel. Together and separately, we **(2)** _____ (visit) some really exciting places. My parents **(3)** _____ (be) to Peru many times. They **(4)** _____ (see) Machu Picchu and **(5)** _____ (walk) the Inca Trail. My brother and I **(6)** _____ (go)

to Europe a couple of times. We **(7)** _____ (kayak) on fjords and **(8)** _____ (ski) on glaciers in Scandinavia. And my sister and I **(9)** _____ (take) the train from London to Paris.

We **(10)** _____ (never, travel) to Japan, so I **(11)** _____ (not, eat) 'real' sushi, and I **(12)** _____ (not, be) able to see the cherry trees in bloom. I **(13)** _____ (not, go) to Africa yet either. I **(14)** _____ (always, want) to go on safari and see lions and giraffes.

17 Complete the questions with the correct form of the verbs in brackets.

1 _____ you _____ (ever, read) about people in Lhasa sticking out their tongues? It's a polite greeting there.

2 _____ they _____ (not, tell) you about the *mano*? That's where young Filipinos sometimes press the hand of an older person to their own forehead. It's very polite.

3 _____ you _____ (not, see) people touching each other's feet in India? It's a greeting called the *pranāma*.

4 _____ anyone _____ (do) the *kunik* with you in Greenland? People put their nose and top lip on your cheek and breathe in. It's a special way of greeting someone there.

5 _____ you _____ (rub) noses with anyone? For traditional Bedouins, it is a respectful greeting.

6 _____ you _____ (hear) people clap to greet each other? That's what the Shona people in southern Africa do.

7 _____ you _____ (not, ever, notice) people raising their eyebrows as a greeting? They do that in the Marshall Islands.

8 _____ you _____ (not, say) that you went to Niger? Then you probably saw people shaking their fists near their heads and saying 'Wooshay!' to greet each other.

5B Coming of age

VOCABULARY BUILDING Suffix -al

1 Complete the sentences. Change the nouns in brackets to adjectives ending in -al.

1 Going walkabout is an important _____ tradition among the Yolngu people. (culture)

2 A _____ walkabout can last for up to six months. (tradition)

3 Going walkabout can be a very _____ experience for a boy. (emotion)

4 Songs and singing are part of the _____ aspect of going walkabout. (music)

5 Boys going walkabout are surrounded by _____ sights and sounds. (nature)

6 Uluru, or Ayers Rock, is a very famous sandstone rock in one of Australia's _____ parks. (nation)

READING

2 Read the text and complete the summary with the correct words.

| aboriginal | ancestral | desert |
| grandfather | skills | tradition |

It is a/an **(1)** _____ for some young Australian **(2)** _____ boys to go walkabout for up to six months, completely on their own and without supplies. A walkabout is a journey that reminds the boys of similar journeys that they believe their **(3)** _____ spirits made thousands of years ago. The boys follow songlines that help them find their way through the Australian **(4)** _____. Sometimes, the boys travel part of the walkabout with a male relative, for example, their father or **(5)** _____. They need to develop many important **(6)** _____ in order to survive the walkabout.

3 Choose the correct answer to the questions.

1 How long have the Yolngu people lived in Australia?

  a 10,000 years
  b hundreds of years
  c over 50,000 years

2 What is the aboriginal term for an invisible pathway that crosses the land?

  a song
  b songline
  c ritual

3 According to the Yolngu, who created the songlines they follow?

  a ancestral spirits
  b Australians
  c outsiders

4 How long does a walkabout last?

  a six months
  b twelve to thirteen years
  c 1,000 days

5 What is the main reason for going walkabout?

  a to make maps
  b to look for footprints
  c to survive alone in the desert

6 Who might teach a Yolngu boy about his ancestral songlines?

  a his grandfather
  b his sister
  c his aunt

4 Are the statements true (T), false (F) or is the information not given (NG)?

1 The Yolngu are an aboriginal group that has lived in Australia for tens of thousands of years. _____

2 Songlines are pathways that are visible to anyone in the desert. _____

3 The Yolngu believe that ancestral spirits look after the boys while they go walkabout. _____

4 A Yolngu boy usually learns his clan's songlines from his father, grandfather and other male relatives. _____

5 Yolngu girls learn about their ancestral songlines from their mothers and grandmothers. _____

6 Going walkabout is one way that Yolngu boys demonstrate that they're ready to take on new responsibilities. _____

Going walkabout

1 🎧 54 Imagine waking up in the morning alone, hundreds of miles away from anyone you know, with no supplies, in the middle of a desert. This is what one day of 'going walkabout' is like for a young Yolngu, or Australian aboriginal*, boy. The Yolngu have lived in Australia for approximately 60,000 years. In fact, they and other aboriginal people lived on the continent of Australia for tens of thousands of years without seeing people from any other places. The land was theirs. As a result, they respect tradition and have a strong connection to the land.

2 One of their oldest traditions is called 'going walkabout' in English. The Yolngu and other aboriginal clans, or family groups, believe that invisible trails, called songlines, cover the land. According to their beliefs, songlines are secret pathways that follow the journeys made by ancestral* spirits as they created the earth. These ancestors sang names for everything that crossed their paths and, in the process, created and named everything in the world. Aboriginal people consider songlines to be the footprints of their ancestors.

3 Going walkabout is a coming-of-age event for twelve- to thirteen-year-old aboriginal boys. When young males go walkabout, they follow the songlines of their ancestors. They sing traditional songs in order to navigate, or find their way, as they walk. And they often walk very far. Some boys travel up to 1,000 miles, without any supplies, in the six months of a typical walkabout! They need to develop important skills in order to make the journey. The goal of going walkabout is to be able to survive alone in the wild just as their ancestors did.

4 Before they go walkabout, boys learn about songlines from the older people in the clan. Some walk parts of their ancestral songlines with their father, grandfather, or another male relative or friend. They learn to use songlines as a kind of map. They use the songs to identify parts of the landscape, such as caves or hills, and to connect to the stories that their ancestors have told for thousands of years.

5 When the boys return from going walkabout, they celebrate with their families and friends. They have made the passage from childhood into the adult world. They have already proved that they can take care of themselves during the six months of going walkabout and that they're ready for new responsibilities.

aboriginal *belonging to the race of people who were living in Australia before Europeans arrived*

ancestral *related to people in your family who lived long before you*

5C Stop me if you've already heard this one

GRAMMAR Present perfect with *for, since, already, just* and *yet*

1 Complete the sentences with these words. In some sentences there may be more than one correct answer.

already	for	since	yet

1 A Do you want to go to the gym with me this afternoon?

B No, I've _____ been there this morning.

2 He hasn't called his brother _____ last month.

3 Natalie has studied _____ three hours.

4 A Did you hear Aunt Sofia is coming to visit next week?

B Yes! I've _____ heard the news.

5 A Have you started your English homework _____?

B Actually, I have _____ finished it.

6 A Have you asked your teacher for help _____?

B No, I haven't asked him _____. I think I'll talk to him tomorrow.

7 Arata has lived with his cousins _____ two years.

8 Yasmin has _____ celebrated her *fiesta de quince años*.

2 Underline the present perfect verbs.

Do you know that humans aren't the only species that has rich social lives and family ties? For example, chimpanzees do as well. How do we know this? Well, have you ever heard of Jane Goodall? She is a scientist who has studied chimpanzees since 1960. She has learned a lot about chimpanzees since then. And she has shared this knowledge with both the scientific community and the rest of the world. For example, Goodall has taught us that not only do chimpanzees have rich social lives and family ties, they also make and use tools. She has set a very high standard for studying apes in the wild and has focused on individual characteristics as well as group patterns.

3 Match the questions with the answers.

1 Is the plane here yet? _____
2 How long have you taken English classes? _____
3 Do you know my friend Tammy? _____
4 Have you tried some of this pizza yet? _____
5 How long has your brother worked at that company? _____
6 How long have Shen and Jun been friends? _____
7 Have you finished your essay? _____

a He has been there since 2015.
b Yes, I've already eaten some.
c They met in 2011 and have been friends ever since.
d No, I haven't met her yet.
e Yes, I've just handed it in to our teacher!
f Yes, it's already arrived.
g I've studied English for two years.

4 Put the words in the correct order to make sentences and questions.

1 called / three times / has / already / She

_____ .

2 the test / Have / yet / for / revised / you

_____ ?

3 got / I've / from school / just / home

_____ .

4 been / never / The students / to another country / have

_____ .

5 we haven't / We have / met / cousins / that / even

_____ !

6 since / has studied / 2017 / Jana / English

_____ .

7 for / my best friend / Renato / five years / has been

_____ .

5 Answer the questions so they are true for you. Write complete sentences.

1 Have you learned to drive yet?

_____

2 Have you already done your homework for this week?

_____

3 What is something you have just finished doing?

_____

4 How long have you been a student at this school?

_____

5 Have you ever visited an English-speaking country?

_____

6 What is one food you have never wanted to eat?

_____

7 How long have you known your best friend?

_____

8 Have you been on holiday this year?

_____

6 Use the prompts to write sentences or questions with the present perfect. You may need to add words.

1 I / live Bangalore / for / three years

_____ .

2 I / already / listen that song / twice

_____ !

3 She / not / go rock climbing / since / last year

_____ .

4 Alex / be / my friend / since / four years old

_____ .

5 We / just / go / beach

_____ .

6 Nate / already / eat breakfast

_____ .

7 They / just / finish / take test

_____ .

8 I / not talk / new neighbour / yet

_____ .

9 How long / you / know / Jack and Sally

_____ ?

7 Choose the option which is closer in meaning to the original sentence.

1 I've just taken a walk.
  a I took a walk not long ago.
  b I have been taking walks for a long time.

2 Niko's teacher was surprised to find out he had already learned about ancient Roman history.
  a Niko's teacher was surprised he had studied history.
  b Niko's teacher didn't expect him to know about ancient Roman history.

3 He's lost his book.
  a He doesn't have his book now.
  b He lost his book, but has it now.

4 I haven't learned all of the new vocabulary yet.
  a I did not learn all of the new vocabulary, but I plan to soon.
  b I did not learn all of the new vocabulary and I am not planning to.

5 He has just come from Dubai.
  a He recently arrived from Dubai.
  b He arrived from Dubai more than a month ago.

6 It's 2018 now and Kim has known Eliza for four years.
  a Kim met Eliza in 2014.
  b Kim knows Eliza now, but didn't know her in 2014.

7 She hasn't made plans for after graduation yet.
  a She knows what she's doing after she graduates.
  b She doesn't know what she's doing after she graduates.

8 My cousins have already seen the film.
  a My cousins saw the film.
  b My cousins did not see the film.

8 Choose the correct response for each question.

1 How long have you had that phone?
  a I've had it for last week.
  b I've had it since last week.

2 Do you know how to get to the art museum?
  a No, I don't. I haven't been there for I was a child.
  b Yes, I've been there regularly since I was a child.

3 Have you seen the new painting at the museum?
  a No, I've seen it already.
  b Yes, I've already seen it.

4 Did you talk to Tavish yesterday?
  a No, I haven't talked to him since last week.
  b Yes, I have talked with him yesterday.

5 Have you started your piano lessons yet?
  a Yes, I've already started my lessons.
  b Yes, I've just been started my lessons.

6 How long have you played the piano?
  a I was playing the piano for 2009.
  b I began playing when I was six years old.

7 Have you invited your teammates to the party yet?
  a No, I haven't invited them yet.
  b Yes, I have invited them yet.

8 Do you know Sarah?
  a Oh, yes, I've known her for a long time.
  b Oh, yes, I've already known her.

5D Why we laugh

TEDTALKS

AUTHENTIC LISTENING SKILLS

1 Listen to the TED Talk extracts and complete each sentence with the correct word or short phrase.
🎧 55

1 Sophie noticed laughter when she was a
_____.

2 She saw her parents doing something
_____ when they were laughing.

3 They were _____ with laughter. She didn't know what they were laughing at, but she wanted to join in.

4 Her parents were laughing at a _____ that people used to sing.

5 The song _____ around signs in toilets in trains.

6 She says that the English have a sophisticated
_____.

WATCH ▶

2 Watch the TED Talk and choose the correct answers to the questions.

1 Who thought that humans were the only animals that laugh?

 a Sophie Scott
 b Robert Levenson
 c Nietzsche

2 What does Sophie say about laughing with other people?

 a People aren't really laughing at jokes.
 b People laugh less when they are with other people.
 c People make other people laugh with jokes.

3 What do people try to show when they are laughing in a group?

 a that they think things are funny
 b that they are part of the group
 c that they have feelings

4 What is *posed laughter*?

 a when someone laughs because something is funny
 b when someone laughs at a silly song
 c when someone makes a fake laugh

5 How does laughter affect relationships?

 a It helps people become less stressed.
 b It makes people annoyed.
 c It makes people speak better.

6 What does Sophie say about laughter?

 a It is a new and recent behaviour.
 b It is an ancient and evolutionary behaviour.
 c It is something humans do to be different from other animals.

3 Are the statements true (T) or false (F)?

1 Laughter is most similar to human speech. _____
2 Laughter sounds like animals calling each other. _____
3 Humans are the only animals that laugh. _____
4 People are more likely to laugh if they are with other people. _____
5 Laughter is a social interaction or activity. _____

4 Match the words with the definitions.

1	social	**a**	a group of animals that includes humans
2	laughter	**b**	something that involves other people
3	voluntary	**c**	connected with feelings
4	involuntary	**d**	making a person laugh
5	emotional	**e**	an act or something people say which makes people laugh
6	funny	**f**	the sound of a laugh
7	joke	**g**	when someone does something without being asked
8	mammals	**h**	when someone does something because he can't control himself

VOCABULARY IN CONTEXT

5 Choose the correct words to complete the sentences.

1 My parents thought the song was really _____. They laughed really hard.
 a silly   **b** frightening   **c** beautiful

2 When people laugh, they make _____ sound. It isn't a usual sound.
 a a silly   **b** an odd   **c** a stupid

3 I cared about laughter and when I became a neuroscientist, I cared about it again. It's a _____ thing to care about. Not many people care about it.
 a scary   **b** dangerous   **c** weird

4 I wanted to find out the beginnings of laughter. The _____ of it.
 a origins   **b** ending   **c** sounds

5 Laughter has two different _____. There are two causes for it.
 a problems   **b** meanings   **c** roots

5E Invitations

SPEAKING

1 Listen and complete the conversations with the correct words. 🎧 56

1 **A** Hey, Marta, _____
_____?

B _____. Why?

A Well, I'm having a party at my house. Can you come?

B Oh, _____.
What time should I come over?

A Any time after 8.

2 **A** _____?

B _____. I usually spend time with my family in the afternoon.

A Well, a few of us are going cycling. Want to come?

B Um, _____.
Can I let you know later?

A Yeah, just text me, OK?

3 **A** Jane, have fun playing at the concert tonight!

B Thanks! Would you like to come and hear the band?

A _____.

B No problem.

4 **A** Hey, listen. _____?

B _____. Why?

A There's this new skate meet at the youth club.

B Oh, yeah? _____.

A It starts at 7.

B Cool! I'll be there!

5 **A** Hey, Lucy! I just wondered, you haven't replied to my invitation to see the play my brother's starring in.

B Oh, yeah, _____.
One sec.

A Sure.

B Yeah, I thought so. _____
_____.

A Oh, that's a shame.

2 Find and correct the mistake in each sentence. Then decide the function of the sentence or question. Write the letter on the line.

(A) asking if someone is available
(S) saying if you are available or not
(Y) accepting an invitation
(N) saying no to an invitation

1 Are you near next Saturday?
_____

2 I need to make my schedule.
_____

3 Sure, I love to.
_____

4 She depends.
_____

5 This sounds great!
_____

6 Thanks for inviting me, but I'm worried I'm busy.
_____

7 I'll go to ask my parents.
_____

8 Are you making anything on Tuesday night?
_____

9 Sorry, I can't take it, but thank you for inviting me.
_____

10 Are you above on Sunday?
_____

11 I (don't) think that.
_____

12 I'm not definitely.
_____

3 Describe an invitation you got recently.

You should say:
- who gave you the invitation
- how you know them
- what the invitation was for
- how you responded to the invitation
- why you gave this response.

You will talk about the subject for one to two minutes. Record yourself. Take one minute to think about what you're going to say. You may make notes to help you. Then listen and compare your recording with the model answer. 🎧 57

WRITING Informal invitations and replies

4 Write the missing letters of the following abbreviations.

1 A__A__   as soon as possible
2 __S__P   reply and say if you can make it
3 __S   let me also add this

5 Complete the text with the correct words. There is one word you don't need.

| apologize | begin | date | enjoy |
| know | make it | offer | say |

> When you write an invitation, you should include the time, **(1)** _____, location and type of event. Remember to ask the person to let you know if they can come.
>
> When you accept an invitation, **(2)** _____ by thanking the person who invited you. Ask any questions you might have about the event. You could also **(3)** _____ to bring something (food or drinks, for example).
>
> If you can't go to the event, you should still **(4)** _____ *thank you* for the invitation. Then **(5)** _____ and, if you want to, you can give a short explanation about why you can't **(6)** _____. It's polite to end by saying you hope they **(7)** _____ the event.

6 Read the invitation. Then circle the information that answers the questions below.

> Jason,
>
> I'm having a surprise party for Pablo on Sunday the 18th from 7pm to 10pm at the tennis club. We're celebrating his success at the tennis finals last weekend. Can you make it?
>
> RSVP
> Mike

1 Who is the invitation to?
2 What kind of party is it?
3 Who is the party for?
4 What day and date is the party on?
5 What time does the party end?
6 Where is the party being held?
7 What is the reason for the party?
8 Who is sending the invitation?

7 Read the note. Then put the points in the correct order.

> Hi Boris,
>
> Thanks for inviting me to the street party on Friday. It sounds like fun, but I'm really sorry, I can't make it. I've already made plans with my cousin. (We're going to a concert in town.)
>
> Hugo
> PS I hope everyone has a fantastic time at the street party!

_____ hopes people enjoy the street party
_____ explains why he can't go
_____ gives a greeting
_____ says *no* to the invitation
_____ apologizes
_____ says *thank you* for the invitation

8 Imagine you are Pat. This is an invitation you have received from your friend, Erika.

> Hey Pat,
>
> I'm having a dinner party on Thursday the 9th at 7:30 at my house. I'm going to cook curry and rice. Can you make it?
>
> RSVP
> Erika

Write a note to Erika accepting or saying no to the invitation. Include the following information:

If you can make it
- thank the sender for the invitation
- say you can make it
- offer to bring something
- ask a question

If you can't make it
- thank the sender for the invitation
- say you can't make it
- explain why
- say you hope the party goes well

Review

1 Unscramble the words for family members and other people.

1 onrmadhretg _____
2 rgantres _____
3 scamletsa _____
4 tessir _____
5 nuta _____
6 nulce _____
7 robhert _____
8 scunoi _____
9 ruoighenb _____
10 etametam _____

2 Complete the sentences with the correct words.

1 Your mother's sister and brother are your _____ and _____.
2 Your mother's brother's children are your _____.
3 If your parents have other children besides you, they are your _____ and _____.
4 Your father's mother and father are your _____ and _____.
5 People that you don't know are _____.
6 People you go to school with are your _____.
7 People you play sports like football or hockey with are your _____.
8 Waving, shaking hands, kissing, hugging and bowing are all ways to _____.

3 Correct the present perfect mistakes in the sentences.

1 Scientists have document multi-generational family groups of elephants which have up to twelve members and are led by the oldest female. _____
2 Researchers has observed wolves giving up their own lives to protect other wolves in their pack. _____
3 Young orcas that scientists have studying spend their entire lives with their parents in the wild. _____
4 People has spot dolphins that tried to save people from shark attacks. _____
5 Scientists have notice that female lions lick other lions, both male and female, to strengthen the social bonds in their group. _____

6 Researchers have make videos of chimps grooming each other, which is important for maintaining chimp 'friendships'. _____
7 Zookeepers has noticed that Asian small-clawed otters spend nearly all their time together – even when they sleep! _____

4 Put the words in the correct order to make sentences and questions.

1 I / minutes / ridden / bike / just / for / my / have / fifteen

_____
_____.

2 She / party / already / has / planned / the

_____
_____.

3 new / a / He's / built / just / house

_____
_____.

4 already / from / She's / university / graduated

_____
_____.

5 in / long / How / you / lived / Denmark / have

_____
_____?

6 long / London / How / has / at / school / in / she / been

_____
_____?

7 she / yet / on holiday / been / Has

_____
_____?

8 have / We / since / children / they / Alice and Rosie / were / known

_____
_____.

5 Choose the correct option to complete the sentences.

1 He hasn't written his essay *yet / just*.
2 She has lived with her sister *for / since* seven months.
3 Connie has *yet / already* practised the piano.
4 He has *since / just* read the letter from his grandfather.
5 She's watched that TV show *for / since* it began.
6 They *had travelling / have travelled* to Mexico every summer since they were eight years old.
7 Marty *is feeling / has felt* sick for three days.
8 Anna and Colin have lived in Liverpool *already / for* fifteen years.

6 Do your best

6A The best I can be

VOCABULARY Goals and expectations

1 **Revision** Choose the correct words to complete the sentences.

1 Riko enjoys meeting new people. She's very *worried / relaxed / friendly*.
2 The students are quiet because they are *nervous / relaxed / afraid* about the test.
3 Ana is *relaxed / afraid / shy* to fly.
4 They are *friendly / shy / worried* about money.
5 Alana was *nervous / relaxed / friendly* during her holiday. She enjoyed it.
6 Rafael doesn't talk in class because he's *relaxed / friendly / shy*.
7 Jake is really *angry / excited / afraid* with me because I forgot to call him.
8 He never helps clean the flat. He's incredibly *upset / pleased / lazy*.

2 Complete the table with these words.

accept	accepting	fail	failed
failure	imperfect	imperfection	perfect
perfection	reject	succeed	success
successful	unsuccessful		

Positive	Negative

3 Match the two parts of the sentences to complete the definitions.

1	Something **perfect**	**a**	is a bad result.
2	When something **fails,**	**b**	is not perfect.
		c	it finishes without success.
3	A **success**	**d**	you think it's OK.
4	Something that has **imperfections**	**e**	you don't think it's OK.
		f	has a good result.
5	When you **accept** something,	**g**	has no mistakes or problems.
6	A **failure**		
7	When you **reject** something,		

4 Complete the table with these words.

accept	fail	failure	imperfect
imperfection	perfect	perfection	reject
succeed	success	successful	unsuccessful

Noun	Verb	Adjective

5 Complete the sentences with the correct form of *be, have* or *have to*.

1 You don't have to _____ perfect. Just try your best.
2 Don't buy that mirror. It _____ an imperfection in the glass.
3 The brothers opened a restaurant last year, but it _____ unsuccessful and it closed.
4 Jake, you _____ accept it. Your vision _____ imperfect. You need glasses!

5 She didn't get into the team. Now she thinks she _____ a failure.

6 This _____ perfect! I want to buy it.

7 She _____ a successful design business in the city.

8 It was difficult at first and they _____ work very hard to make the project a success.

6 Choose the correct option to complete the sentences.

1 The students work hard in order to _____.
  a perfection **b** success **c** succeed

2 Sometimes it's hard to _____ failure.
  a accept **b** imperfect **c** reject

3 The worst _____ is to not try.
  a success **b** failure **c** imperfection

4 People have different ideas about what it means to be _____.
  a succeed **b** perfection **c** successful

5 Young people often feel a need to be _____.
  a imperfect **b** perfect **c** succeed

6 You can learn from _____, but you can also learn from failure.
  a success **b** successful **c** perfect

7 Remember that nobody's _____.
  a perfect **b** imperfect **c** accepting

8 People who always look for _____ will be unhappy.
  a failure **b** imperfection **c** perfection

7 Listen and write the correct word to complete each sentence. 🎧 58

| accept | failure | imperfect | imperfections |
| perfect | reject | successful | |

1 Teachers _____ that students will make mistakes as they learn English.

2 But some students do not accept their own _____ English.

3 They think making mistakes means _____.

4 They don't want to speak until their English is _____.

5 These students need to _____ the fear of failure and start talking.

6 _____ students work hard and try to learn from their mistakes.

7 The best way to improve _____ is to practise.

8 **Extension** Choose the correct words to complete the sentences.

1 She owns a very *successful* / *success* / *accepting* company.

2 My friend had a bad week. He *failed* / *rejected* / *succeeded* two exams.

3 Buy this fruit. It costs less because it has *perfect* / *imperfect* / *imperfections*.

4 This author's first book was very *successful* / *perfect* / *accepting* and it made her famous.

5 An apple is a *perfect* / *successful* / *failed* example of a healthy snack.

6 Items such as clothing and furniture that are slightly *failed* / *imperfect* / *rejected* usually cost less.

7 I was locked out of my phone after three *unsuccessful* / *imperfect* / *accepted* attempts to unlock it with my code!

8 Studying in an English-speaking country is a(n) *perfect* / *successful* / *accepted* opportunity to improve your English.

9 I'm really disappointed because the university *accepted* / *succeeded* / *rejected* my application.

9 **Extension** Put the words in the correct order to make sentences.

1 car / in / condition / is / father's / My / perfect

_____
_____.

2 Miguel's / rejected / group / idea / The

_____
_____.

3 skiing / winter / Minato / attempt / at / last / made / unsuccessful / an

_____
_____.

4 more / success / Is / or academic / economic / important

_____
_____?

5 actions / accept / have to / responsibility / for / their / They

_____
_____.

6 a / Kanna / example / a / of / student / hard-working / perfect / is

_____
_____.

PRONUNCIATION Reduced *have to* and *has to*

10 Listen and underline the reduced forms you hear. You will not underline words in every sentence. 🎧 **59**

1 Students have to show a student ID to enter the library.
2 Lucas doesn't want to work today, but he has to.
3 No, you don't have to complete the essay today.
4 I don't have to get up early, but I do.
5 Turn off your phone now. Everyone has to.

LISTENING

11 Listen to the conversation. Answer the questions. 🎧 **60**

1 Why is the man going to the museum?
  a for a project
  b for fun
  c for his art class
  d for his job

2 What is the problem?
  a He is busy on Saturday.
  b He can't get to the museum.
  c He doesn't like art museums.
  d He isn't a good student.

3 What does the man have to do?
  a choose a gift in the gift shop
  b choose a painting or sculpture and draw it
  c choose a museum to go to
  d choose a piece of art and write about it

12 Listen and answer the questions. 🎧 **61**

1 Where would you hear this announcement?
  a on the radio
  b on television
  c in school
  d in a supermarket

2 What is the purpose of the announcement?
  a to provide information about closing time
  b to give a weather update
  c to report on road conditions
  d to say that the wifi is not working

3 When will the place open again?
  a after the snow stops
  b after tomorrow
  c before Thursday
  d after 3pm tomorrow

13 Listen and choose the correct option to complete the sentences. 🎧 **62**

1 According to the fruit seller, the fruit is _____.
  a perfect
  b imperfect
  c damaged

2 The fruit arrangement includes _____.
  a an orange
  b a banana
  c an apple

3 There are two kinds of _____.
  a apple
  b melon
  c pear

4 The type of container chosen is a _____.
  a box
  b basket
  c bowl

5 The customer wants a gift sent to _____.
  a his home
  b Chicago
  c Macedonia

6 The bowl is _____.
  a imperfect
  b traditional
  c perfect

7 The price includes _____.
  a an additional bowl
  b free delivery
  c insurance

14 Listen to the conversations. Answer the questions. 🎧 **63**

1 How do the speakers describe the vegetables?
  a perfect
  b not perfect
  c expensive

2 What is the student asking about?
  a a class
  b a text
  c a test

3 What are the speakers talking about?
  a weekend plans
  b success stories
  c travel

4 How was the woman's presentation?
  a a failure
  b perfect
  c unsuccessful

GRAMMAR Modal verbs: obligation, prohibition, permission, advice

15 Match the statements with the instructions or information.

1 You can't talk in this room.
2 You can't pay with a credit or debit card.
3 You must be a student to enter the library.
4 I have to finish my homework today.
5 I should go to a tutor for help with my English.

a Students must hand in their essays tomorrow.
b Students only. Please show your ID.
c Quiet, please!
d Tutors available Tuesday and Thursday afternoons.
e Cash only.

16 Read each sentence. Change the modal verb to rewrite it as a negative sentence.

1 At our school students have to wear a uniform.
_____

2 Students should use social media every day.
_____

3 Our coach says we must eat just before a match.
_____

4 You have to have a password to use the wifi.
_____

5 We have to be quiet.
_____

6 I can call you tonight.
_____

7 You should close your social media account.
_____

8 Students have to pay to use the pool.
_____

9 They can take drinks into the classroom.
_____

17 Complete the sentences. There may be more than one correct answer.

can	can't	don't have to	have to
must	should	shouldn't	

You **(1)** _____ follow these rules in yoga class. You **(2)** _____ wear shoes in the yoga studio. Leave your shoes outside. You **(3)** _____ use a yoga mat, but you **(4)** _____ bring your own. You **(5)** _____ use the mats the studio provides. You **(6)** _____ talk in the yoga class. You **(7)** _____ be quiet. You **(8)** _____ wear comfortable clothes. You **(9)** _____ try to do exercises that you're not ready for. You **(10)** _____ be patient. Yoga takes practice!

18 Complete the sentences with the correct modal verb. There may be more than one correct answer.

1 It's going to rain. You _____ take an umbrella.
2 At this restaurant you _____ wear jeans.
3 You _____ pay to visit the museum. It's free for students.
4 You _____ bring a small gift for your friend's parents.
5 Football players _____ wear any jewellery during the match.
6 People _____ turn off their phones in the theatre.
7 Customers _____ use the café's wifi. It's free.
8 No, you _____ learn German. You should study English instead.

19 Choose the correct modal verbs to complete the sentences. Choose all answers that are correct and logical.

1 You _____ be seventeen years old to have a driving licence.
   a must   b have to   c should

2 You _____ text Antonio and ask him to give you a lift to school.
   a couldn't   b should   c can't

3 Students _____ use their phones during the exam.
   a can't   b don't have to   c must not

4 She _____ read more books in English.
   a should   b can   c must not

5 In my opinion, restaurants _____ waste food.
   a shouldn't   b can't   c should

6 You _____ talk on the phone in the cinema.
   a don't have to   b must not   c can't

7 When you don't understand something, you _____ ask a question.
   a should   b must not   c don't have to

8 You _____ take photos in the museum.
   a have to   b can   c must

9 If you want to be successful, you _____ work hard in class.
   a should   b can't   c don't have to

6B Finding new ways

VOCABULARY BUILDING Negative prefixes

1 These words and the prefixes in the table form opposite words. Complete the table with the words.

active	agree	connect	correct
direct	finished	honest	kind
like	lucky	mature	~~perfect~~
proper	successful		

dis	im	in	un
	perfect		

READING

2 Read the text. Are the sentences true (T), false (F) or is the information not given (NG)?

1 The museum exhibit is unusual. _____

2 The exhibit includes perfect and imperfect items. _____

3 A coin that is not round might be something you could find on display in this museum. _____

4 All of the imperfect items are valuable. _____

5 The exhibit shows that *perfect* means the same thing to all cultures. _____

6 Artists had to reject items that were unusable. _____

7 The exhibit shows that all imperfections are mistakes.

_____

3 Read the text again and choose the correct options.

1 The meaning of the word *circular* in paragraph 2 is similar to
   a whole.
   b metal.
   c silver.
   d round.

2 In paragraph 2, why does the author include information that the imperfect items were found in many parts of the world?
   a to provide evidence that the items are from more than one culture
   b to show that the exhibit is international
   c to encourage people from all over the world to see the exhibit
   d to explain why some items are glass and others are metal

3 Which of the following can be inferred from paragraph 3?
   a *Perfect* and *imperfect* mean the same in all cultures.
   b The creators of the exhibit believe it is better to fail than to succeed.
   c The creators of the exhibit believe that people learn from failure.
   d Something that is imperfect can still be useful.

4 The meaning of the word *process* in paragraph 3 is similar to
   a routine.
   b procedure.
   c result.
   d instruction.

5 According to paragraph 3, all of the following statements are true of the imperfect items EXCEPT:
   a Unusable items were rejected.
   b Imperfect small statues were accepted.
   c Imperfect coins were usable and accepted.
   d Imperfect items had no value.

6 According to paragraph 4, what happened to make the items imperfect?
   a The artist made the imperfections on purpose.
   b Something damaged them after they were made.
   c A mistake made them all the wrong colour.
   d Imperfect items are important in the artists' cultures.

7 The meaning of the word *deliberate* in paragraph 4 is similar to
   a intentional.
   b unintentional.
   c unsuccessful.
   d delicate.

4 Match the causes with the effects.

1 In the process of making these items, something went wrong.

2 Some imperfect items were unusable.

3 Some imperfect items, like coins, were acceptable.

4 Some cultures think imperfection is acceptable.

a People used them.
b Artists made imperfect items on purpose.
c They're imperfect.
d The artists rejected them.

Less than perfect

1 🔊 **64** Museums are famous for their great works of art. Perfect sculptures, paintings and treasures from ancient times are what people expect to see. Usually. But one museum has an unusual exhibit of items that are imperfect. It's called 'Less than perfect.'

2 Some of the imperfect items are coins that are not circular, bottles that bend to one side and ceramic pots that are thin on one side and thick on the other. These items are failures. Some objects in the exhibit are more than 2,000 years old, but others are more recent mistakes. They were found all over the world and now are at the Kelsey Museum of Archaeology at the University of Michigan in the US.

3 There are two important parts to the exhibit. The first is 'Failed perfection'. It includes imperfect bowls, glass, small statues, coins and other objects. In the process of making these items, something went wrong and the result was imperfections in the product. The artists had to reject some things because they were unsuccessful and unusable. For example, a bowl with a crack in it or a bottle that formed without a bottom. But other imperfect items, such as small statues and coins with the image not in the centre, were acceptable and people used them.

4 The second part is called 'Deliberate imperfection'. With these items, the artists made them imperfect on purpose. This was often for cultural reasons. For example, some Japanese pottery from five hundred years ago has flaws* on purpose because of the idea that there is beauty in imperfection.

5 The museum shows these imperfect objects to make people think about what *perfect* meant to other cultures in different times. And to think about what people learned from these failures.

flaw *mistake, imperfection*

6C Unexpected art

GRAMMAR Zero conditional

1 Listen and complete the sentences. 🎧 65

1 When you try hard, you _____.
2 If you learn to drive, you _____ my car.
3 If you listen carefully, you _____ a lot.
4 If you don't work hard, you _____ the test.
5 When people exercise, their health
_____.
6 When I buy fruit at the farmer's market, it
_____ better.
7 When I watch films in English, I _____
new vocabulary.
8 When he doesn't get enough sleep, he
_____ very rude.

2 Complete the text with the correct phrases.

a painting party is	If someone needs a break,
if the painting isn't perfect,	they laugh about it with a friend
they often share a photo of	
it online	

If you want your friends to spend time together,
(1) _____ a good idea. It's creative and fun.
A teacher gives instructions, but nobody's work is a failure.
When people make mistakes, **(2)** _____.
They accept imperfections. **(3)** _____ he/
she can have something to eat or drink and chat with others.
It is a party after all. When people finish a picture,
(4) _____. And **(5)** _____
they still share it!

3 Match the two parts of the sentences.

1 If you fail, _____
2 When you iron your clothes, _____
3 When Emilio cooks, _____
4 If a player scores a goal, _____
5 When you come to my house, _____
6 If she drinks too much coffee, _____
7 When the baby cries, _____
8 When his phone rings, _____

a they look better.
b you can meet my family.
c Jun looks to see who is calling before he answers.
d try again until you succeed.
e she feels nervous.
f the food is very spicy.
g the game is over.
h his mother picks him up.

4 Read the text. Find six mistakes and correct them.

If you use social media be careful about what you post. For
example, when you are posting photos, think about the
other people in the photos. If they don't want the photo
online, you shouldn't to post it. If you post comments
don't write anything inappropriate or unkind. When you
receive a friend request from someone you don't know
don't accept it. If you want to keep your information
private, you can to change the settings. And when you are
online too much, you take a break for a day or two.

5 Listen. In each sentence, underline the clause in which
you hear rising intonation. 🎧 66

1 If you want to relax, you should watch a good film.
2 When you're in the cinema, you can forget other things
and enjoy the film.
3 If you like films, go to the film festival.
4 When you're at a film festival, you should see several films.
5 If you watch a film in English, you can learn new
vocabulary.

6 When you see a film you like, you should tell your friends to see it.

7 When you see a film you don't like, you should tell your friends not to see it.

6 Choose the correct words to complete the paragraph.

When you're in London, *take / taking* a walk through Harrod's food hall. It's a world of speciality food. Sometimes *when / if* you walk through the hall, you *can / can't* try samples, like a piece of chocolate or a taste of meat or cheese. The large hall and the foods are beautiful. Just looking is almost as good as eating. But, if you have a camera, you *shouldn't / don't* use it. Photography is not allowed.

7 Put the words in the correct order to make sentences. In sentences where the comma is not present, the result clause comes first.

1 Lima / Miraflores neighbourhood / to / you / the / Go / when / to / go

_____.

2 phone / If / turn off / your / relax, / want / you / to

_____.

3 stand / I / take / always / When / the / I / bus,

_____.

4 comes / news / watches / my / When / he / father / home, / the

_____.

5 I / my / family / coffee / I / make / get up / for / when

_____.

6 a / If / make / are / sandwich / you / hungry, / you / can

_____.

7 try / If / flavour / ice cream, / like / you / this / should / you

_____.

8 you / you / a test, / talk / test / If / fail / during / the

_____.

8 Use the prompts to write advice with the zero conditional.

1 If / go / Barcelona / should / visit / the Pedrera
   *If you go to Barcelona, you should visit
   the Pedrera.*

2 If / like / sweet things / try / some churros

_____

3 When / arrive / take / walk / along / Las Ramblas

_____

4 should / take photos / if / visit / the Sagrada Familia

_____

5 If / love / seafood / take / metro / restaurant in Barceloneta

_____

_____

6 should / go / beach / when / want / relax

_____

_____

9 Complete the sentences using the zero conditional with your own ideas.

1 If you don't try to speak English, _____

_____.

2 When you travel overseas, _____

_____.

3 If you visit my city, _____

_____.

4 When you visit my country, _____

_____.

5 If you like art, _____

_____.

6 When you don't succeed, _____

_____.

7 If you like something, _____

_____.

8 When you don't like something, _____

_____.

6D Teach girls bravery, not perfection

TEDTALKS

AUTHENTIC LISTENING SKILLS

1 Complete the extracts from the TED Talk with words or phrases that mark contrast. Then listen to check your answers. 🎧 67

1 For years, I had existed safely behind the scenes in politics as a fundraiser, as an organizer, _____, I always wanted to run.

2 She had never lost a race and no one had really even run against her in a Democratic primary. _____, this was my way to make a difference, to disrupt the status quo.

3 The polls, _____, told a very different story.

4 She tried, she came close, _____, didn't get it exactly right.

5 It turns out that our girls are really good at coding, _____ just to teach them to code.

6 We have to show them that they will be loved and accepted not for being perfect _____ for being courageous.

WATCH ▶

2 Watch the TED Talk and complete the sentences with the correct words.

accepted	brave	failed	perfect
risk	socialize	trial and error	win

1 My pollsters told me that I was crazy to run, that there was no way I could _____.

2 It was the first time in my entire life that I had done something that was truly _____, where I didn't worry about being _____.

3 Most girls are taught to avoid _____ and failure.

4 It's often said in Silicon Valley, no one even takes you seriously unless you've had two _____ start-ups.

5 Coding, it's an endless process of _____, of trying to get the right command in the right place, with sometimes just a semicolon making the difference between success and failure.

6 We have to _____ our girls to be comfortable with imperfection and we've got to do it now.

7 We have to show them that they will be loved and _____ not for being perfect but for being courageous.

3 Put the sentences in the correct order.

_____ The coding teachers notice that the girls feel they have to be perfect.

_____ Saujani ran for Congress, but was unsuccessful.

_____ Saujani wants girls to learn to code and to be comfortable with imperfection.

_____ She started a company to teach girls to code.

_____ Saujani says that girls are taught not to take risks.

4 Choose the correct words to complete the sentences.

1 Writing computer code is a process of trial and error. It is *easy / difficult* to get it right at first.

2 Girls often *delete / correct* their code when it has mistakes.

3 Boys usually say, 'There's a problem with *me / my code.*'

4 Girls usually say, 'There's a problem with *me / my computer.*'

5 Good coders are *perfect / brave*.

6 Saujani thinks we should *be comfortable with / fight* imperfection.

VOCABULARY IN CONTEXT

5 Complete the sentences with the correct words.

courageous	negotiate	potential	ran
struggling	supportive network		

1 She _____ for Congress, but she didn't win.

2 People have to learn to _____. It's a skill that takes practice.

3 When students move to another country to study, it's hard because they don't have a _____ in the new place.

4 My teacher says I have the _____ to do better in this class.

5 It's more important to be _____ than perfect.

6 I'm really _____ with this homework.

6E Giving advice

SPEAKING

Useful language

Giving advice

If someone asks for advice, use these expressions.

*When you don't understand something in class, **you should** ask your teacher for help.*
*If you need more maths practice, **try** downloading a maths app.*
Why don't you…?

The best time to give advice is when someone asks for it. If someone hasn't asked, but you want to give advice, be polite and use these expressions.

*If the computer isn't working, **you might want to try** re-starting it.*
*I can see you don't have a phone signal. I got a signal near the window and **that may work for you**.*
*I'm not sure, but I think this door is locked after 6:00. **You may/might** need to use the side entrance.*

1 Complete the conversations with words and phrases from the Useful language box. More than one answer may be possible. Then listen and check your answers. 🎧 68

1 A How can I get better at this video game?
  B _____ watch some online tutorials?
2 A I'm really worried about cooking dinner for everyone this weekend.
  B _____ you aren't confident in the kitchen, _____ asking someone for help.
3 A I always know exactly where I'm going.
  B _____ this is the wrong way. _____ need to go back to the main road.
4 A This is useless. I can't do it!
  B _____ you're not sure about the answer, _____ checking it with someone.
5 A Oh, no! I'm going to look so stupid. Everyone else is so much better than me!
  B You look a bit nervous. I think about my breathing when I'm nervous and _____.
6 A I've just failed my driving test. What am I going to do?
  B _____ you don't succeed at something, _____ try to do it again.

2 Listen to the sentences in Exercise 1 again. Underline the words that have a higher pitch. Listen to the example. 🎧 69

Example: A *There's <u>nothing</u> to do!*
  B *If you're <u>bored</u>, you <u>could</u> help me clean the house.*

3 Read the advice. Decide if the other person asked for the advice (Y) or not (N).

1 If the homework is too difficult, try asking for some help. _____
2 If the bus is late, you might want to try checking the app. _____
3 Why don't you Google it? _____
4 I found a great price when I searched online, that might work for you. _____
5 I'm not sure, but I think you need to reserve a seat. You might want to check. _____
6 When you go to South America, you should visit Machu Picchu. _____

4 Read the situations and make notes about what advice you would offer. Use the Useful language. Then listen to the model answers and compare your ideas. 🎧 70

1 You are waiting at a bus stop. Some tourists are talking about where they can go for lunch.
2 An online friend talks to you about her problems with her brother/sister. They are often unkind and they argue a lot.
3 You reply to a post on social media asking what music is popular in your country.
4 Some people visiting your town are planning to go to the local museum tomorrow, but that's the day when it's usually closed.
5 A student from another country is coming to stay with your family for a week. Think about some useful advice you can give them.

WRITING An advice blog

5 Read and label the advice blog.

a conclusion   **b** problem   **c** topic
d solution 1   **e** solution 2   **f** solution 3

_____ It's good to have goals.

_____ You might have personal goals, like travelling or learning a new language, and, of course, academic and professional goals are also important. But goals can cause problems, too. Some people worry so much about their goals that they forget about everything else. This can be unhealthy. If you have a goal that is taking up all of your time, here is some advice that might help.

_____ Think about what really matters in your life, for example, your family and your friends. While you are working on your goal, make sure you still see the people who care about you. Focusing on your goals and nothing else could make you very lonely.

_____ It may sound obvious, but don't forget to eat well and sleep enough at night. If you're putting all of your energy into your goals so that you miss meals and go to bed too late, you could become unwell. Take care of your health and well-being!

_____ Keep a positive attitude about your goals, but try to have another plan in case something goes wrong. It's normal to feel disappointed when we don't reach our goals, but it's important not to become too upset. After all, there are always other things you can do.

_____ Remember, goals are great, but we all need a healthy balance between living well and working toward our goals.

6 Read the advice blog in Exercise 5 again. Are the statements true (T) or false (F)?

1 The blogger doesn't think that people should have goals. _____

2 According to the blog, it's a problem when we focus too much on our goals. _____

3 The blogger advises people not to spend too much time with their family and friends. _____

4 The blog reminds people to eat and sleep well while working on their goals. _____

5 When we don't reach our goals, we shouldn't feel disappointed. _____

6 The blogger's conclusion is that it's best to have a balanced approach to our goals. _____

7 Complete the text with the correct words or phrases.

a problem	advice	costs nothing	don't worry
for free	good news	no problem	too expensive
too much	wonderful		

Money gives us the freedom to do many things. But not having enough money is **(1)** _____ that many of us live with. However, there is some **(2)** _____. Follow this **(3)** _____ and soon you'll find yourself enjoying the things you thought you couldn't afford!

All your friends are members of a gym and they go to lots of cool classes. The fees are too high for you? **(4)** _____. Exercising in nature **(5)** _____ and anyway is more fun. Invite your friends to join you for a run on the beach or a bike ride in the park. Have fun!

You love the theatre, but tickets cost **(6)** _____? No problem. Volunteer or get a part-time job working at a theatre a couple of evenings a week. The work isn't difficult and you'll get to see the shows **(7)** _____. Enjoy!

Everyone is talking about this beautiful restaurant in town, right? You want to go, but it's **(8)** _____. No problem. Most restaurants offer special deals that don't cost very much, especially in the middle of the week. Check it out!

So, if you don't have much money, **(9)** _____. It's still possible to do many **(10)** _____ things!

8 Choose one of the problems. Then follow the instructions.

Everyone I know is really into sports. I mean, everyone in my family and all my friends either watch sports or play sports, or both. The problem is that I have absolutely no interest in sport. I find it boring. What can I do? —*Tomas*	*I got my driving licence last month, which is great. The problem is now everyone expects me to drive them everywhere! I don't mind helping sometimes, but my friends are always asking me to take them places. What should I do?* —*Yumi*

Write a paragraph offering advice for one of the problems. Suggest at least three solutions.

- Confirm what the problem is.
- Establish why it is a problem.
- Offer some solutions.
- End with a concluding sentence.

9 Write about the following topic.

> Guido has very good neighbours, but one drops by to visit much too often and another parks her car on Guido's drive.
>
> What are the problems and solutions?

Give reasons for your answer and include any relevant examples from your own knowledge or experience.

Write at least 250 words.

Review

① Put the words in the correct order to make sentences.

1 the / for / gift / shopping / girlfriend / perfect / for / my / I'm

_____ .

2 the / didn't / failed / and / revise / He / test

_____ .

3 films / actor / was / The / two / in / unsuccessful

_____ .

4 today / is / perfect / weather / The

_____ .

5 in / is / nature / perfection / There

_____ .

6 made / he / The / a / pie / success / was

_____ .

7 it / product / fix / This / claims / skin imperfections / can

_____ .

8 afraid / to / fail / be / Don't

_____ .

② Match the word or phrase with the meanings.

1 courageous
2 negotiate
3 potential
4 ran
5 struggling
6 supportive network

a discuss and make compromises
b people that care about you and help you
c ability
d tried to win an election
e having difficulty
f brave, not afraid

③ Use the prompts to write complete sentences.

1 turn off / phones / in school

_____

2 not / wear / trainers / restaurant

_____

3 need to / charge / phone

_____

4 buy tickets / for / before Saturday

_____

5 not / use phone / in

_____

6 go home / before / dark

_____

7 be / eighteen / to

_____

8 not text / teacher

_____

9 password / use / wifi

_____

④ Complete the descriptions with your own ideas.

Example: If something is perfect, _people like it_.

1 When someone is confident, _____

_____ .

2 If a sports team is successful, _____ .

3 If the students are hard-working, _____

4 When a person is lazy at the weekend, _____

_____ .

5 I accept help from others when _____

_____ .

6 She feels brave when _____

_____ .

7 A project fails when _____

_____ .

8 When I don't succeed at something, _____

_____ .

⑤ Write a paragraph with some advice to a student who started learning English recently. In your paragraph, use modal verbs, the zero conditional and vocabulary from the unit.

_____

_____

_____

_____

_____

_____

_____

_____

_____

_____

_____

_____

_____

_____

_____

_____

_____

_____

7 Tell me what you eat

7A Food and flavours from around the world

VOCABULARY Food, drink and flavours

1 **Revision** Listen and match the descriptions with the images. 🎧 71

a

b

c

d

e

f PIZZA

1 _____   4 _____
2 _____   5 _____
3 _____   6 _____

2 **Revision** Listen again. Complete the sentences with one word in each gap. 🎧 71

1 The meal they are talking about is _____. He had juice with this meal today.

2 She drank _____ and ate _____ this morning.

3 He's having some _____ and a _____ for _____ today.

4 He's going to have _____ and salad for _____.

5 She usually has _____ and _____ in the evening.

6 He doesn't think it's a good idea to have _____ later because of the _____.

3 For each item, write one word from the list that describes it.

dessert	drink	meat	salty
sour	spice	vegetable	

1 lemon _____
2 potato _____
3 curry _____
4 crisps _____
5 tea _____
6 ice cream _____
7 chicken _____

4 Complete the sentences with the correct words.

1 I want to cook something spicy. Do we have any c_____ p_____?

2 Wild fruits are the best. The s_____ in our garden are small, dark red and very sweet.

3 Sandwiches often come with f_____ f_____ in restaurants, but you should order a salad instead. Salad is less salty and much better for you!

4 A_____ grow on trees and they can be red, yellow or green. They can also be sweet or sour.

5 Many children don't like the flavour of v_____, but they love s_____ things like desserts like i_____ c_____.

6 She likes meat and chicken, but she can't eat fish or p_____. Seafood makes her sick.

7 Ch_____ is a popular ingredient that is used in many desserts and even hot drinks, but without sugar in it, it is actually quite b_____.

5 Choose the correct words to complete the sentences.

1 French fries are made from *potatoes* / *tomatoes*.
2 Mexicans eat a lot of *spice* / *spicy* food.
3 Strawberries are *sweet* / *salty*.
4 Many people enjoy the *flavour* / *snack* of coffee.
5 Coffee is *sour* / *bitter* before you add sugar and milk.

6 Ice cream is a popular *drink / dessert* all around the world.

7 Apples are a very common *fruit / vegetable*.

8 Italian-style *pasta / lemon* with meat and tomato sauce is a very popular meal in many countries.

9 *Prawns / Chickens* come from the sea.

10 Too much *beef / snack* or other red meats is unhealthy.

6 Listen and choose the correct description. 🎧 **72**

1 a She's cooking Indian food.
   b She's making a fruit salad.
   c She's eating a salty snack.

2 a He's going to buy a snack.
   b He needs an ingredient to make dinner.
   c He wants a hot drink.

3 a She doesn't like very spicy food.
   b She loves her friend's cooking.
   c She wants some more chicken.

4 a She's preparing food for a party.
   b She doesn't eat meat.
   c She's ordering sandwiches at a café.

5 a He doesn't like the lunch dishes.
   b He's trying to choose a dessert.
   c He's not very hungry.

6 a She's looking for the meat section.
   b She's looking for the fruit section.
   c She's looking for the snack section.

7 **Extension** Complete the crossword.

Across

1 cheap and quick meal, for example, a burger and french fries (2 words)

5 bad for you

7 cooked using direct heat

8 cooked in hot water

9 cooked in hot oil

Down

1 cold, like ice

2 tastes very good

3 really bad

4 it makes your food spicy (2 words)

6 like vegetables picked from the garden this morning

7 very large

8 **Extension** Choose the correct words to complete the text.

Let's face it – many people today have a pretty **(1)** _____ diet. Lots of people don't take time to eat a good lunch with friends or family. Instead, they get **(2)** _____, which is cheap and often fried or covered with cheese, and they eat it quickly in their cars. They drink coffee or fizzy drinks full of sugar. After work, they are too tired to cook, so they heat up some **(3)** _____ meals from the supermarket. Or they go out to restaurants, where they are served a **(4)** _____ amount of food – and there is often a big dessert after the meal! All of this is **(5)** _____ for the body.

However, things are starting to change. More and more people are interested in changing their habits. They are buying **(6)** _____ fruits, vegetables, meat and eggs from local farms. They're drinking water instead of fizzy drinks. They're looking for restaurants that serve normal-sized dishes with interesting **(7)** _____ and local ingredients. They are discovering that home-cooked meals **(8)** _____, and that **(9)** _____ food is lighter and healthier than **(10)** _____ food.

1 a healthy
   b spicy
   c unhealthy

2 a a home-cooked meal
   b fast food
   c fresh vegetables

3 a frozen
   b amazing
   c boiled

4 a fresh
   b frozen
   c huge

5 a terrible
   b delicious
   c natural

6 a frozen
   b fresh
   c boiled

7 a amounts
   b flavours
   c delicious

8 a taste terrible
   b smell bad
   c taste amazing

9 a grilled
   b salty
   c fried

10 a boiled
   b fried
   c sweet

PRONUNCIATION Minimal pairs

9 Listen and choose the words you hear. Then practise saying the sentences with both words. 🎧 73

1 Are you going to *taste / waste* that food?
2 I think this dish needs more *rice / spice.*
3 *Peas / Bees* are very important on the farm.
4 Can you please pass me that *meat / wheat*?
5 A great way to relax is to *bike / bake.*
6 I don't like the smell of this *beef / leaf.*
7 He made the chicken and vegetables in a *curry / hurry.*
8 I got the recipe from a *cook / book.*

LISTENING

10 Listen and answer the questions. 🎧 74

1 What is a potluck dinner?
   a Everyone cooks the meal together.
   b Everyone brings a dish to the dinner.
   c Everyone tries to guess what the food is.

2 What is the man planning on bringing?
   a a cheesecake
   b a dessert
   c a curry

3 What does the woman think might be funny?
   a if she isn't able to get the organic honey
   b if he doesn't warn people about the spices
   c if they bring the same dish to the dinner

4 What does the woman need for her dish?
   a organic honey
   b cheesecake
   c hot peppers

5 What is the woman definitely going to do?
   a make a dessert
   b make a cheesecake
   c make something spicy

6 What is the woman not sure about?
   a if she'll be able to eat all the spicy foods
   b if other people are bringing dishes to the dinner
   c what she'll make if she doesn't get the honey

11 Listen to the speaker and decide what his philosophy about life is. 🎧 75

a Don't regret the mistakes you've made.
b Be kind to everyone you meet.
c Find something you enjoy and do it.
d Keep calm and carry on.

12 Listen again. Choose the correct answers. 🎧 75

1 What has the young man been wondering about?
   a if he should work in a restaurant or not
   b if he should go to university or not
   c if he should ask his parents for money or not

2 Why does he think some people go to university?
   a because they feel like they're supposed to
   b because that's the best way to get a good job
   c because they'll be disappointed if they don't

3 How long has he worked at the local restaurant?
   a since last summer
   b he hasn't yet
   c for three summers

4 What is he doing this summer?
   a working at the restaurant
   b going to catering college
   c he still isn't sure

5 How long does the catering course last?
   a eight weeks
   b two years
   c eighteen months

6 What is he going to do if he isn't accepted at catering college?
   a think about a different career
   b continue to work towards his career goal
   c apply to a university

7 Why does he feel so lucky?
   a because he has a good job in a restaurant
   b because he is going to catering college
   c because he knows what he wants to do

GRAMMAR Predictions and arrangements

13 Complete the sentences with the correct form of *will* and the verb in brackets.

1 We _____ (not eat) all of this food!
2 The tomatoes _____ (be) ripe and ready to eat in July.
3 Nonno's Pizza, a new restaurant, _____ (open) in two weeks.
4 I _____ (call) the restaurant and book a table.
5 The takeaway delivery _____ (arrive) in 30 minutes.
6 Turn down the heat or the sauce _____ (burn).
7 Friday's newspaper _____ (print) a review of Finn's Café.
8 We _____ (not have) enough time to make a salad.

14 Put the words in the correct order to make questions.

1 we / have / a / Sarah / party / this / Will / year / big / for
_____?
2 family / invite / of / friends / we / her / all / and / Will
_____?
3 the / Will / food / parents / our / prepare / help
_____?
4 help / Ana / with / Will / decorations / the
_____?
5 invitations / Will / by / send / email / the / we
_____?
6 Will / cake / bake / a / David
_____?
7 arrange / Zach / Will / music / dancing / for
_____?

15 Choose the correct option to complete the sentences.

1 One serving of kale *will give / is going to give* you more calcium than a large glass of milk.
2 Eating kale *going to add / will add* fibre, protein, omega-3s, and vitamins and minerals to your diet.
3 One cup of kale *are going to have / will have* only 33 calories and tons of vitamins, minerals and protein.
4 If you buy kale, it *won't to be / isn't going to be* expensive.
5 You can use kale to make lots of things. *You going to want / You'll want* to try it in a smoothie, a salad, a side dish – or baked as a crisp!

6 Adding kale to your diet *won't to cause / is not going to cause* medical problems.
7 If you travel to Scotland, Kenya or Portugal, you *will seeing / are going to see* kale on the menu.
8 The average person in other places *going to eating / will eat* only two to three cups of kale every year.
9 You *will be able / is going to be able* to find kale in your local supermarket.

16 Complete the sentences with the correct form of the verbs in brackets. There may be more than one correct answer.

1 Tonight, the chef _____ (prepare) his favourite meal, spaghetti Bolognese, for us.
2 The sous chef _____ (help) by chopping onions, carrots, celery and tomatoes, and gathering the garlic, rosemary, basil and oregano.
3 The chef _____ (start) by boiling the spaghetti in salted water.
4 Then he _____ (begin) cooking the sauce.
5 He _____ (heat) olive oil in a pan and then cook the onion, carrot, celery, garlic and rosemary for about ten minutes.
6 Then he _____ (stir) in the minced beef and cook it until it's brown.
7 He _____ (add) canned tomatoes, basil, oregano, tomato purée and fresh tomatoes.
8 He _____ (cook) the sauce for about an hour and create a thick, rich sauce.
9 Finally, he _____ (combine) the cooked spaghetti and sauce.
10 He _____ (serve) the spaghetti with grated Parmesan cheese.

17 Use the prompts to write predictions that are true for you. Use *will*, *going to*, *may* or *might*.

1 speak English _____
2 travel to _____
3 meet _____
4 try _____
5 know _____
6 In 5 years, I _____
7 In 10 years, _____

7B The greatest human success story

VOCABULARY BUILDING Suffixes

1 Complete each sentence with the correct form of the word in brackets. Add the suffix *-er, -ment* or *-ance* and make changes to spelling where necessary.

1 What might be some of the consequences of the _____ (disappear) of farming as a way of life?

2 Where will our food come from if fewer people decide to become _____ (farm) in the future?

3 The _____ (develop) of urban and vertical farms will be a big step towards helping to feed people in the future.

4 Being able to grow food indoors for millions of people would be a tremendous _____ (accomplish).

5 Urban farming is an exciting field that brings together plant scientists, architects, urban _____ (plan), engineers and economists.

6 The future of farming is dependent on the _____ (accept) of new ideas and methods.

READING

2 Read the text and choose the correct answer to the questions.

1 Why is urban farming an important development for the future?

  a It's important to control conditions such as carbon dioxide, humidity and light.

  b According to the UN, 6.5 billion people will live in cities by 2050.

  c because shops don't produce the food they sell

  d If farming as a way of life disappears, urban farms will help feed people in cities.

2 What are some advantages of urban or vertical farms?

  a In the near future, twice as many people will live in cities as today.

  b Traditional farming as a way of life is slowly disappearing.

  c You can control light and water, and you don't have to worry about weather or insects.

  d A personal food computer keeps track of conditions such as carbon dioxide levels, humidity and light intensity.

3 How is aeroponic farming different from traditional farming?

  a Both aeroponic and traditional farmers need to worry about insects, weather and light conditions.

  b Engineers, architects, urban planners, economists and plant scientists all work together on aeroponic farms.

  c Unlike traditional farms, aeroponic farms can control growing conditions 365 days a year.

  d Aeroponic farms will be one way you'll get at least some of your food in the future.

4 How do plants in a food computer receive nutrients?

  a A food computer is a climate-controlled box.

  b Sensors in a food computer keep track of humidity and light.

  c Aeroponically grown plants don't need sunlight.

  d They're fed by a mist that includes necessary minerals.

5 Why are vertical farms able to provide food exactly where it's needed?

  a because plants in vertical farms don't need sunlight

  b because vertical farms can be located in cities

  c because not all of our food comes from shops

  d because vertical farms work 365 days a year

3 Choose the correct heading for each paragraph.

1	Paragraph 1	**a**	Urban farms of the future
2	Paragraph 2	**b**	Who will feed the future?
3	Paragraph 3	**c**	Aeroponic farming
4	Paragraph 4	**d**	Aeroponics and you!
5	Paragraph 5	**e**	Personal 'food computers'

4 Match the words with the definitions.

1	estimate	**a**	a chemical substance found in nature
2	mineral	**b**	a person who has scientific training and who designs and builds complex structures
3	root		
4	factory		
5	climate	**c**	to make an informed guess
6	vertical	**d**	the typical weather in a place
7	row	**e**	going up and down rather than from side to side
8	engineer	**f**	the part of a plant that grows below the ground
		g	a building in which products are made
		h	a group of objects arranged in a line

Urban farms: the future of food?

1 🎧 **76** Do you know where your food comes from? Does it matter to you? If you live in a city, you probably get most, if not all, of your food from shops. Of course you know that shops don't produce the food they sell. Farms do. But did you know that farming as a way of life is slowly disappearing? The United Nations estimates that by 2050, 6.5 billion people will live in cities. (That's about twice as many as today.) If fewer and fewer people become farmers, where is our food going to come from?

2 Caleb Harper, a National Geographic Explorer, has an idea. Caleb thinks that people should grow food near the places they live and not just on traditional farms. He's part of a new movement that hopes to see 'urban farms' and 'vertical farms' in cities in the not-too-distant future. Caleb's organization is the CityFARM research group. CityFARM brings together engineers, architects, urban planners, economists and plant scientists to study alternatives to traditional farms.

3 One of the tools Caleb is interested in developing is what he calls a 'personal food computer'. A food computer is a small box with plants inside it. The food computer has sensors* that measure conditions such as carbon dioxide levels, humidity and the amount of light. There's no soil. The plants get nutrients* through a mist, a fine spray of water, that has minerals added in.

4 This type of farming, in which plant roots are fed by mist and not grown in soil, is called aeroponics. Now picture a type of aeroponic food computer that's as big as a warehouse*. In here, plants grow without soil or sunlight. All of the plants are fed aeroponically (by mist) and the climate is controlled. There's no risk of storms, cold weather or droughts. Insects can't harm the plants. The system works 365 days a year, day and night. That's more or less what a vertical* farm is like.

5 Because vertical farms can be built in cities, inside old warehouses or factories, or even on top of schools, they can provide food exactly where it's needed. Whether it's a personal food computer designed to grow your favourite vegetables in your home or a vertical farm in an urban apartment building, aeroponic farming will probably be one of the ways you get at least some of your food in the future.

sensors *devices that respond to heat, light, pressure, etc.*
nutrients *substances that plants, animals and people need to live and grow*

warehouse *a large building used for storing goods*
vertical *up and down instead of side to side*

7C A taste of honey

GRAMMAR First conditional

1 Listen and complete the sentences. 🎧 77

1 _____ you go walking in Arizona, _____ need to wear sunscreen.

2 You _____ lose your work _____ you don't save your files every ten minutes.

3 _____ you water your plants every week, _____ be healthy and beautiful.

4 I _____ get my driving licence in the autumn _____ I take driving lessons this summer.

5 You _____ wear your blue suit _____ you go to your cousin's birthday.

6 _____ I leave my hat by the pool, my sister _____ get it for me.

7 It _____ be difficult to do well in your exam _____ you play video games all afternoon.

2 Listen and complete the sentences with the correct word or punctuation. 🎧 78

1 _____ you go walking in the desert _____ you might see some interesting wildlife.

2 I might have to go to summer school _____ I fail the exam.

3 I may go rock climbing _____ I visit Chamonix.

4 _____ you stay out on the beach too long _____ you could get sunburnt.

5 _____ we don't pay the rent _____ our landlord may be upset.

6 I may eat tacos _____ I go to that new Mexican restaurant.

7 _____ we leave before breakfast _____ we might arrive on time.

3 Tick the sentence in each pair that is more certain.

1 _____ If the flat is dirty, Chris may clean it.

_____ When the flat is dirty, Chris will clean it.

2 _____ He will do yoga and meditation when he is upset.

_____ If he is upset, he might do yoga and meditation.

3 _____ When you learn to swim, you'll go to the pool more often.

_____ You may go to the pool more often if you learn to swim.

4 _____ If you listen to this music, you may love it!

_____ You'll love this music when you listen to it!

5 _____ Khalid won't come with me when I go to the cinema on Saturday.

_____ Khalid might not come with me if I go to the cinema on Saturday.

6 _____ When I go to Canada, I won't visit Toronto.

_____ I might not visit Toronto if I go to Canada.

7 _____ When you go to the meeting with your teacher, she'll help you with your essay.

_____ If you go to the meeting with your teacher, she may help you with your essay.

8 _____ I could have a banana and some tea if I get hungry on my flight.

_____ When I get hungry on my flight, I'll have a banana and some tea.

4 Choose the correct words to complete the sentences. There may be more than one correct answer.

1 *If / When* you like Spanish food, you might want to make a *tortilla*.

2 *If / When* you want to make one, you'll need to buy a lot of eggs.

3 *If / When* you go to the supermarket, you'll also need to buy potatoes, olive oil and an onion.

4 *If / When* you cut the onion, it *might / will* make you cry.

5 When the olive oil is hot, it *may / will* be time to add the onion and potato.

6 *If / When* the onions and potatoes are cooked, you'll need to add the egg.

7 When you flip the tortilla, you *might / will* drop it. Be careful!

8 *If / When* you eat it, you might want to serve a small salad or some bread as well.

9 *If / When* you're trying to lose weight, you won't want to eat too much!

5 Choose the correct option to complete the sentences.

1 I *eat / ate* hummus and tabbouleh when I want to be really healthy.

2 If I learn to swim, *I'll go / I'll to go* to the pool every day.

3 If we go into town for the match, we *could / if* go to that new restaurant for lunch.

4 I *won't / could* buy any cheese when I go to the supermarket.

5 If you go outside tonight, you might *see / seeing* the full moon.

6 Remember you could call your cousin *won't / if* you need help.

7 If you drive too fast, you may *get / got* a speeding fine.

8 When it's raining tomorrow, you *might want / will want* to go to the cinema.

9 I might *to go / go* shopping today if I leave work early.

6 Complete the second sentence so that it means the same as the first. Use no more than three words in each sentence.

1 I may win the contest and, if that happens, I will get a prize.

_____ I win the contest, _____ get a prize.

2 It's possible that you will not go to the party with Mary and, if that happens, she will be upset.

If you _____ go to the party with Mary, _____ be upset.

3 Sometimes I go to bed at 8:00 and, when I do, I am happy when I wake up.

_____ I go to bed at 8:00, I _____ up happy.

4 We are going to the beach in July and, when we do, it's possible I will go diving.

_____ we go to the beach in July, I _____ go diving.

5 He could be late and, if he is, he'll call to tell you.

_____ he's _____ to be late, he'll _____ to tell you.

6 We may see the play on Saturday, but if we don't see it, we won't have a chance to see it again.

If we _____ see the play on Saturday, we _____ it at all.

7 I could read the lesson ahead of time and, if I do, I might answer more questions in class.

I _____ answer more questions in class _____ I read the lesson ahead of time.

7 Read the questions. Choose the correct answer.

1 When will you pay me back if I lend you money?
   a If you lend me money, I will pay you back next week.
   b I might pay you back next week when you are lending me money.

2 When she goes to Paris, what will she do?
   a She might visit the Eiffel Tower when she's in Paris.
   b If she goes to Paris, she may visit the Eiffel Tower.

3 If you buy a new car, will it cost a lot of money?
   a I won't buy a new car if I may not have a lot of money.
   b If I buy a new car, it may cost a lot of money.

4 Did you talk to Rob today?
   a No, I didn't. But I may speak to him later if I go to science club.
   b No, I didn't. When I go to science club, I won't speak to him.

5 Will your mother be annoyed if you don't go on holiday with your parents this year?
   a Yes, if we wouldn't go, she could be annoyed.
   b Yes, if we don't go, she'll be annoyed.

6 When you walk along the river this afternoon, will you bring a book to read?
   a Yes, I may bring a book when I walk along the river.
   b Yes, if I bring a book, I will walk along the river.

7 Have you mown your lawn yet this year?
   a Yes, when it's sunny and warm last week, we could need to mow it.
   b No, but if it's sunny and warm next week, we may need to mow it.

8 Complete the sentences with your own ideas using the first conditional.

1 If I eat a lot of junk food, _____

_____.

2 When I have time to cook dinner, _____

_____.

3 If I don't have time to cook, _____

_____.

4 I go to restaurants _____

_____.

5 When I want something sweet, _____

_____.

6 If I eat dinner with my family, _____

_____.

7 When I eat with my friends, _____

_____.

7D The global food waste scandal

TEDTALKS

AUTHENTIC LISTENING SKILLS

1 Listen to TED Talk extracts and choose the correct answer to the questions. 🎧 79

1 What do you think Stuart is going to talk about next?
- **a** He will explain his life story.
- **b** He will explain surplus.
- **c** He will explain why people get hungry.

2 What do you think Stuart is going to talk about next?
- **a** why he likes to shop at big supermarkets
- **b** what he found was being thrown away
- **c** the things he bought at the supermarket

3 What do you think Stuart is going to talk about next?
- **a** why biscuits are delicious
- **b** how biscuits are made
- **c** how biscuits connect to food waste

4 What do you think Stuart is going to talk about next?
- **a** how supermarkets are a part of wasting food
- **b** why supermarkets are doing a great job
- **c** why people should shop at supermarkets

5 What do you think Stuart is going to talk about next?
- **a** how people should get jobs as farmers
- **b** how farmers waste food
- **c** how farmers are losing their jobs

WATCH ▶

2 Watch the TED Talk. Choose the correct option to complete the sentences.

1 Stuart believes the solution to food waste is to simply *sit down and eat / throw away* food.

2 The wasted food that Stuart is talking about is *rotten / good, fresh* food.

3 People *cut down forests / make more supermarkets* to grow and farm more food.

4 Food goes to waste even before it leaves *the fields / people's houses*.

5 Corporations need to *grow their own food / tell people* what they are throwing away.

6 There are 13,000 slices of fresh bread thrown away in one factory in *one year / one day*.

3 Tick the things that Stuart says contribute to food waste.

1 the public _____
2 hungry people _____
3 animal food _____
4 the planet _____
5 farmers _____
6 corporations _____
7 supermarkets _____
8 lack of refrigeration _____

4 Match the words with the correct paraphrased line from the talk.

1 depend on
2 crust
3 unacceptable
4 symbol
5 hobby
6 very large quantity
7 demonstrate

- **a** Food is being wasted on **an enormous scale**.
- **b** These biscuits **represent** the global food supply.
- **c** I need **to show** you where the food ends up.
- **d** I inspect bins **in my free time**.
- **e** Who eats the **first and last slice** of bread in a loaf?
- **f** We throw away food that hungry people **need**.
- **g** We can stop food waste if we say that **it isn't OK**.

VOCABULARY IN CONTEXT

5 Complete the sentences with the correct words.

global	households	invested
resources	tackle	

1 Stuart wants us to imagine that the nine biscuits that he found in the bin represent the _____ food supply.

2 He thinks people who live in most _____ don't eat the crust – that slice at the first and last end of each loaf.

3 The farmer has _____ £16,000 in growing spinach.

4 He says people have the power to stop this awful waste of _____.

5 The global quest to _____ food waste has started.

7E What's it like?

SPEAKING

Useful language

Making suggestions

How about…?
I think we should have…
We could cook…
Why don't we ask people to bring…?
Why don't we…?
Maybe we should…
What about…?

Describing food

It's a kind of…
It's popular in…
It's really good with…
It's a little salty / fairly sweet / kind of sour / delicious.

Making decisions

We'll have plenty of (pizza) and (salad).
I'll put that on the invitation.

① Listen and complete the sentences. 🎧 80

A What are we going to do to celebrate the end of term?

B (1) _____ go bowling?

C Maybe, but not everyone likes it.

A (2) _____ a Hollywood party?

B What's that?

A (3) _____ film party where everyone dresses up as celebrities or movie characters.

C That's a great idea. And a few of us are DJs, so we can put some music together.

B We'll have plenty of music.

A And **(4)** _____ popcorn… and nachos to eat.

C Do you put meat on your nachos?

A I make nachos with tortilla chips, guacamole, chilli con carne, sour cream and cheese. So **(5)** _____, a little **(6)** _____ and **(7)** _____ with the cream too. **(8)** _____!

B Yeah, **(9)** _____ party food.

A And **(10)** _____ lots of people because you use the tortilla chips like a spoon, so you don't need knives and forks.

C That sounds great.

B (11) _____ the chilli at my house.

A And we'll need lots of tortilla chips, so **(12)** _____ them?

B Great idea.

C This party's going to be awesome!

② Read the three situations below. What suggestions do you have for them?

1 A new friend is coming over to have dinner with your family. She's a vegetarian. What are you going to prepare for dinner?

2 An exchange student wants to know what is one of the most popular foods or meals in your country. Describe it for the student.

3 Your school wants to organize a campaign to reduce food waste in the cafeteria. What suggestions do you have?

For each situation, cover these three points. Make some notes using the Useful language.

• what is/are your idea(s)

_____
_____

• describe the places and things in your idea(s)

_____
_____

• explain why they are good in the situation

_____
_____

③ Imagine that your cousin has just started at a new school and wants to make new friends. Think of suggestions for things your cousin can do to make friends. Make notes on your ideas. Use the Useful language. Then listen to a model answer. 🎧 81

Below are some ideas to help you.

• sports
• study group
• drama group

WRITING A review

4 Choose the correct words to complete the restaurant review.

Eastern Spice is a new **(1)** *restaurant / coffee shop* on the corner of Main Street and Beech Road. It serves excellent Indian food, including curry, naan bread and samosas. The chef grew up in northern India, but has lived in the United Kingdom for many years. He helps his customers to understand how spicy the different **(2)** *countries / dishes* are and encourages everyone to try new **(3)** *flavours / restaurants*. With only eight tables, the place is **(4)** *huge / small* and extremely busy. However, I found it very noisy; the music was much too **(5)** *loud / interesting*! Service is personal with **(6)** *no / lots of* attention to detail, but a little too slow. **(7)** *Prices / Menus* are reasonable… under £15 for two delicious courses! Eastern Spice is open from 6pm to midnight, Tuesday to Sunday. It doesn't open on Mondays. I **(8)** *recommend / like* it for couples or a few friends, but not for large groups.

5 Read the restaurant review again. Then match the questions with the answers.

1 What?
2 What food?
3 Where?
4 When?
5 Closed?
6 Service?
7 Expensive?
8 Recommended?

a Main Street and Beech Road
b 6:00–12:00
c A little slow
d Monday
e No
f Eastern Spice
g Yes
h Indian dishes

6 Read the restaurant review and choose the correct answer to the questions.

P&P is a popular Italian restaurant on Fairfield Avenue, next to the train station. Except Sundays, it's open every day from 12:30 to 10pm and, for dinner, you'll need to book. It's a large, casual place with lots of soft seats and brightly coloured cushions. P&P stands for pizza and pasta, but they also serve salads and grilled meats. Everything is fresh and delicious! Compared to other Italian restaurants, prices are high, but I think it's worth it. The waiters and waitresses are very quick and efficient, and always smiling. I highly recommend it for celebrations and special occasions.

1 Where is the restaurant?
   a in the train station   b on Fairfield Avenue

2 Do you always need to book?
   a just on Sundays   b just for dinner

3 What is the atmosphere like?
   a large   b casual

4 What kind of food do they serve?
   a They serve a variety   b They only serve pizza
      of dishes.   and pasta.

5 Is it expensive?
   a yes   b no

6 How would you describe the service?
   a too slow   b friendly

7 How would you describe the review?
   a mostly positive   b mostly negative

7 Write your own restaurant review. Choose one of the options below. Complete the notes with your ideas, then write your review.

TORO	ZEN
· Spanish restaurant	· Japanese restaurant
· 62 Summer Street	· Lavender Lane
· Mon–Fri, 6pm to _____	· Hours are _____
· Sat & Sun _____	· Chef is from Tokyo
· Dishes include paella and _____	· Atmosphere is stylish and _____
· Prices _____	· Dishes like sushi and _____
· Service is welcoming, but _____	· Very expensive
· Atmosphere is _____	· Service is _____
· Recommend _____	· Recommend _____

8 Read and follow the instructions.
   · The graph below was created by a businessman. It shows the number of customers having meals at sit-down restaurants and fast-food restaurants in his hometown over a period of 30 years.
   · Summarize the information by selecting and reporting the main features, and make comparisons where relevant.
   · Write at least 150 words.

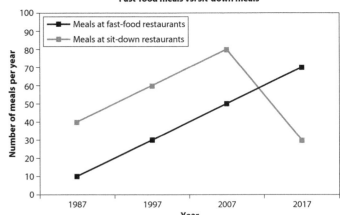

Fast-food meals vs. sit-down meals

Review

1 Unscramble the letters to form the names of foods and drinks.

1 bleastgeve _____

2 fecfeo _____

3 otesmota _____

4 wrarbsetiser _____

5 keccinh _____

6 sranpw _____

7 sapat _____

8 hacolcteo _____

9 yurcr _____

10 febe _____

2 Read the names of the recipes. Match them with the flavour descriptions.

1 Chilli orange chicken with rice _____

2 Hot chocolate with chilli powder, sugar and milk _____

3 Chocolate-covered crisps _____

4 Prawns with lemon pasta _____

5 Hot black tea with sugar and lemon _____

6 Strawberry tart and ice cream _____

7 Dark chocolate cake _____

8 French fries with cheese sauce _____

a It's a dessert that's sweet and a little bitter.
b It's a snack that's salty and sweet.
c It's a dinner with meat and fruit that's salty, sweet and spicy.
d It's a dinner that's salty and a little bit sour.
e It's a warm, salty snack that isn't very light or healthy.
f It's a drink that's sweet and spicy.
g It's a drink that's bitter, sweet and sour.
h It's a sweet fruit dessert.

3 Find and correct the mistakes.

I'm going to make pitta bread with my friends tonight.
(1) Its going to taste so good, because homemade bread is always better than bread from the supermarket.

First we need to get all the ingredients. **(2)** We are need yeast, oil, salt, flour and water. **(3)** Jakob goes to buy the yeast and flour. I've already got the oil and salt.

(4) It taking a while to make the bread, but it's not complicated. **(5)** We're mixing the yeast and flour, and add warm water. After twenty minutes, the dough will rise.

Next, we'll knead the dough and make it into a ball. **(6)** We put oil in a bowl so the dough doesn't stick as it rises. **(7)** That're going to take about two hours.

(8) Then we're going divide the dough into eight equal pieces and roll each one into a ball. **(9)** After half an hour, we are going rolling each ball out until it's a circle about 1/4 inch thick.

Finally, to cook the bread we need to heat a pan and add a little oil. **(10)** We are cooking the bread until it puffs up and turns brown. Then we'll flip it and cook the other side. When both sides are cooked, we'll have delicious bread to eat with dinner!

4 Put the words in the correct order to make sentences.

1 the / They / exam / will / tomorrow / take

_____.

2 When / goes / won't / to / library / , / she / return / her / she / the / books

_____.

3 I / to / take / tomorrow / If / drive / , / will / don't / I / the / bus / school

_____.

4 They're / to / tonight / play / going / together / music

_____.

5 If / follow / might / recipe / taste / his / cake / doesn't / , / the / he / bad

_____.

6 won't / term / next / take / a / Marla / maths / class

_____.

7 chairs / may / come / need / if / We / Anderson and Lea / to / extra / the / meeting / two

_____.

5 Choose the correct option to complete the sentences.

1 If you take the time to learn the new material, *you'll / you won't* do well on the exam.

2 *I'll / I may* be home early if I catch the 4:37 train.

3 She *won't / don't* be in class if she has to go to the doctor's.

4 When I *see / will see* my cousins next month, we might watch a film together.

5 It *might / won't be* rain when I go on my long bike ride tomorrow.

6 If you move to Rome, you might *learn / to learning* Italian.

7 She *may buy / could bought* a dessert if she has enough money.

8 She might *not pass / won't pass* her driving test if she doesn't get more practice.

8 Buyer's choice

8A **Why we buy**

VOCABULARY A product's life

1 **Revision** Label the photos.

department store	price	save money
shop online	shoppers	shopping centre

1 _____

2 _____

3 _____

4 _____

5 _____

6 _____

2 **Revision** Unscramble the words about shopping.

1 raktem _____
2 soctumre _____
3 pesxeivne _____
4 pahce _____
5 ripce _____
6 phogsinp rnecte _____
7 pamdretnet trose _____
8 pends yenmo _____

3 **Revision** Complete the sentences with the correct words.

centre	customer	department	expensive
online	price	sale	save	spend

1 When you buy something, you _____ money.
2 If you buy something at a low _____, then you _____ money.
3 If something is _____, it's not cheap.
4 A shopper is a _____ in a shop.
5 If you don't like to go out shopping, you can shop _____.
6 There are usually lots of shops and a few large _____ stores at a shopping _____.
7 If something is not for _____, that means you can't buy it.

4 Fill in the missing vowels to form words about products.

1 m __ n __ f __ ct __ r __
2 m __ t __ r __ __ l
3 __ pt __ __ n
4 __ dv __ rt __ s __
5 r __ c __ cl __
6 thr __ w __ w __ __
7 d __ s __ gn
8 pr __ d __ c __

5 Match the words with the definitions.

1	throw away	**a**	make in a factory
2	grow	**b**	what something is made of
3	recycle	**c**	choice
4	pick	**d**	put information about a product on TV, radio, in a magazine or online to attract customers
5	manufacture		
6	sell		
7	option	**e**	get bigger
8	advertise	**f**	put in the bin
9	material	**g**	use something again
		h	exchange a product for money
		i	choose

6 Choose the correct words to complete the sentences.

1 You shouldn't *throw away* / *pick* those shoes. They are still good!

2 I want to *recycle* / *sell* my car. How much do you think I can get for it?

3 Our company is *producing* / *growing* fast.

4 I'm not sure which trousers to *pick* / *option*.

5 My friend *designs* / *manufactures* and makes her own dresses.

6 In a large shoe shop, there are always many more *options* / *materials* to choose from.

7 What *manufacture* / *material* is that jacket made of?

8 You know, you should really *recycle* / *throw away* more of your paper and plastic instead of putting it in the bin.

9 Pink just doesn't look good on you. Why don't you *produce* / *pick* a different colour?

7 Complete the conversation with the salesperson's responses (a–f).

A Wow, that's a beautiful bag. Do you know who designed it?

B 1 _____

A What material is that? It looks very unusual.

B 2 _____

A Really? That's interesting! How much is it?

B 3 _____

A Oh, wow. Do you have any less expensive options?

B 4 _____

A Oh. Hmm. That's still a lot of money.

B 5 _____

A That's true. I like that they were not manufactured in a factory. I also like to support local businesses. I didn't even know this shop was here! I just saw it when I was walking by.

B 6 _____

A Well, I will tell all my friends about you. And… I'm sure my beautiful bag will get people's attention. I'll take that one with the pink and yellow design!

a Yes, but remember that these are all produced by hand. They're very special.

b It's made from recycled silk dresses from India.

c You can pick from any of these smaller bags here – they're all £60.

d All of our items are made by local artists.

e Yes, I know. We just opened last month and we need to advertise more!

f I can sell it to you for £100.

8 Complete the text with the correct words.

advertise	design	grown	manufacture
material	option	pick	recycle
sell	throwing		

Online shopping is more popular than ever. Amazon.com has **(1)** _____ into one of the biggest online marketplaces. There, shoppers can **(2)** _____ from millions of products of all kinds – clothes, books, shoes, pet food… pretty much every **(3)** _____ you can imagine!

On the Etsy website, shoppers can find more unique and personal products. Creative, artistic people **(4)** _____ and **(5)** _____ their own items, like jewellery, handbags, t-shirts, decorations and more.

Ebay is another popular site, where people can buy and **(6)** _____ things. It's a great way for people to **(7)** _____ items they don't use any more instead of **(8)** _____ them away. The seller creates a post to **(9)** _____ the item. The post includes photos and a description of the item, including details such as the size, the **(10)** _____ it's made of and the condition it's in.

9 Extension Choose the correct words to complete the sentences.

1 Department stores have many *displays* / *bargains* where they show their products for sale, such as jewellery.

2 *Discount* / *Antique* furniture can be very expensive, especially if it is in good condition and has historical value.

3 Some people don't like online shopping because they don't want to wait for the products to be *delivered* / *displayed* to their house.

4 If you aren't happy with something you've bought, you can usually take it back to the shop and *discount* / *exchange* it for another item.

5 Advertisements are everywhere. They're on TV, on the radio, on the internet and even on giant *bargains* / *billboards* for you to see while you're driving.

6 If something is reasonably priced, that means you can *afford* / *exchange* it.

7 I want to sell my car, so I've posted *an advertisement* / *a display* online.

PRONUNCIATION Compound noun stress

10 Listen. Underline the stressed word in each compound noun. Then practise saying the words. 🎧 82

1 fishnet
2 plastic bags
3 skateboard
4 recycling programme
5 surfboard
6 fishing boat
7 self-esteem
8 electric car

LISTENING

11 Listen to the conversation. Choose the correct answer to the questions. 🎧 83

1 What does the woman ask the man?
  a if he's ever been to Bali
  b if he's seen a certain video
  c if he recycles plastic bags
  d if he has a problem

2 What word does the woman use meaning *to not allow*?
  a prohibit
  b forbid
  c ban
  d disallow

3 What is the problem?
  a Plastic bags are not made on the island.
  b Plastic bags get caught in trees.
  c Plastic bags are more expensive than paper bags.
  d Plastic bags are not recycled.

4 How did the man think about Bali before this conversation?
  a an island with environmental problems
  b an island with great natural beauty
  c an island with far too many tourists
  d an island with a lot of manufacturing

5 What does the Balinese economy depend on?
  a plastic bags
  b tourism
  c exports
  d recycling

6 What does the woman think is very inspiring?
  a people who are tough
  b people in beautiful places
  c people in TED Talks
  d people who take action

7 What do the man and woman decide to do?
  a find a way to get more involved in their community
  b find a way to support the Wijsen sisters
  c find a way to start a recycling programme in their community
  d find a way to travel to Bali

8 What word does the man use meaning *pride in yourself*?
  a self-respect
  b self-worth
  c self-serving
  d self-esteem

A plastic bag floats in the sea.

12 Listen and choose the correct answer to the questions. 🎧 84

1 What do some people call the Great Pacific Garbage Patch?
  a Waste Island
  b Treasure Island
  c Trash Island

2 What has brought all the rubbish together?
  a ocean currents
  b different countries
  c fishing nets

3 Where does the rubbish come from?
  a Texas in the United States
  b North America and Asia
  c a huge garbage patch

4 What is the biggest part of the rubbish?
  a plastic bottles
  b plastic fishing nets
  c plastic bags

5 Why is plastic such a problem?
  a It's biodegradable.
  b It's recyclable.
  c It's not biodegradable.

6 Why does the speaker think countries aren't paying attention to the problem?
  a The problem is far away.
  b The problem is too big.
  c The problem can't be solved.

7 What advice does the speaker give?
  a Never, ever use plastic.
  b Buy reusable materials.
  c Support 'green' companies.

GRAMMAR Second conditional

13 Tick the sentences that include the second conditional.

1 Shops are designed to make you want to buy things. If shoppers like the music in a shop, they are more likely to go in it and buy its products. _____

2 If the music the shop played were slow, people would walk more slowly – and buy more! _____

3 If you wanted to visit all the shops in the largest shopping centre in the world, you would need many, many hours. _____ It has 1,200 shops!

4 If you work at the West Edmonton Mall, the largest shopping centre in North America, you have 23,000 colleagues. _____ It has 800 shops, a water park, restaurants and other exciting tourist attractions.

5 If people think online shopping is 'greener', they will be wrong. _____ One study showed that the negative effects of transporting goods bought online is greater than people expect.

6 If shopping centres had external windows and clocks, people would be aware of how long they had been there. _____ So designers design shopping centres without them!

7 If you wanted to try on every pair of shoes in Selfridges in London, you would put on thousands of pairs of shoes. _____ Selfridges has more than 100,000 pairs of shoes at any time!

8 If people go to a shopping centre, they'll often buy lots more things than they planned to buy when they left home. _____

14 Match the two parts of the sentences.

1 If I found a watch,
2 I would not be late all the time
3 If I weren't late,
4 I would get more job offers
5 If I received several job offers,
6 If I were able to choose the best job,
7 I would be able to buy a watch
8 If I bought a watch,

a I would earn more money.
b if I earned more money.
c if I had a watch.
d I would return the watch I found!
e I would make a better impression.
f I would know what time it is.
g I would choose the best job.
h if I made a better impression on people.

15 Choose the correct verb forms to complete the sentences.

1 He *will bought / would bought / could buy* new clothes if he *save / saved / would save* his money.

2 If our mother *taught / teached / would taught* us how to sew, we *make / could make / made* our own clothes.

3 If the company *not manufactured / did not manufacture / manufactured not* enough smartphones, the price *increased / would increase / would increased*.

4 The shops *are / were / would be* full of unwanted merchandise if no one *buyed / would bought / bought* new clothes.

5 I *would save / saved / would saving* time if I *would shop / shopped / go shop* closer to my home.

6 If the shopping centre *has / will have / had* better shops, we *would spend probably / would probably spend / spend probably would* more money there.

7 If the bookshop *offers / would offer / offered* more interesting books, I *found / would find / would found* one I like.

8 More people *will eat / ate / would eat* at the restaurant if it *would served / served / serves* better food.

16 Combine the two sentences using the second conditional.

Example: We often buy things we don't really need. We don't have a lot of money in the bank.
If we didn't buy things we don't really need, we would have more money in the bank.

1 Shoppers have so much choice. It can be overwhelming.

_____

_____

2 We order shoes and sweaters online. They need to be shipped to our homes.

_____

_____

3 Some people feel better after buying something new. They buy lots of unnecessary things.

_____

_____

4 Personal shoppers aren't cheap. Very few people are able to hire them.

_____

_____

5 Shops aim to sell what they think people want. They make a lot of money doing this.

_____

_____

6 Designers are so creative. They are able to come up with some amazing things.

_____

_____

8B Saving the surf

VOCABULARY BUILDING Compound nouns

1 Complete the sentences with the correct words.

air pollution	billboards	rainforests
sea life	shopping centre	supermarket
TV shows	video games	website

1 Advertisements on _____ are surprisingly effective.

2 This is one of the most difficult _____ I've ever played!

3 There are three _____ about pirates on tonight!

4 A good _____ usually includes a variety of shops.

5 Learning how to create a _____ is a very useful skill.

6 _____ is harmful to people, animals and plants.

7 Fruit and vegetables are usually displayed at the front of a _____.

8 Plastics in the ocean are causing great harm to _____.

9 As many as 30 million species of plants and animals live in tropical _____.

READING

2 Read the text and write the correct word for each definition. There are two words you don't need.

advertiser	aware	awkward
brand	experiment	product
teenager	TV show	video game
website		

1 a person between the ages of thirteen and nineteen _____

2 someone who tries to sell things through advertising _____

3 an electronic game with a screen _____

4 knowing about something _____

5 a programme you watch _____

6 several internet pages linked together _____

7 something that is made and sold _____

8 not relaxed or confident _____

3 According to the text, is each sentence correct (C) or incorrect (I)?

1 Teenagers know exactly what they want. _____

2 Advertisers try to get teenagers' attention in order to sell things to them. _____

3 Brands take advantage of teenagers' feelings of insecurity. _____

4 Teenagers trust advertisers. _____

5 Product placement is only on TV advertisements. _____

6 Teenagers are not influenced by advertising. _____

4 Read the text again and choose the correct options.

1 Advertisers and marketers consider _____ to be an important demographic.

  a peers   **c** marketers

  b teenagers   **d** television characters

2 The meaning of the phrase *figuring out* is similar to

  a thinking about.   **c** trying on clothes.

  b describing problems.   **d** making new friends.

3 According to the text, what about teenagers do advertisers try to appeal to?

  a their insecurities   **c** their friends

  b their budgets   **d** their size

4 According to paragraph 2, which of the following is <u>not</u> true about teenagers?

  a Many teenagers feel insecure.

  b Most teenagers want to fit in with others.

  c Most teenagers are aware of the importance of peer groups.

  d Most teenagers want others to be good-looking.

5 The meaning of the word *scenery* is similar to

  a character.   **c** instrumental music.

  b background.   **d** props.

6 Which of these statements does the writer agree with?

  a Parents have a big influence on what teenagers want to buy.

  b Advertisers have a big influence on what teenagers want to buy.

  c Older teenagers have a big influence on what younger teenagers want to buy.

  d TV characters have a big influence on what teenagers want to buy.

7 Look at the four squares (■) that show where the following sentence could be added to the text. Where would the sentence fit best?

They're aware that most teenagers really want to avoid ever looking awkward.

  a ___   **b** ___   **c** ___   **d** ___

Do you buy it?

1 🎧 **85** Do you like to go shopping? Do you shop only for things you need or do you sometimes shop for things you want but can't afford? Have you ever felt like buying something because you wanted to fit in? If you answered 'yes' to any of these questions, then you're just like a lot of other young people! Young people between the ages of thirteen and nineteen are one of the biggest demographics* out there for marketers and advertisers. (a) [■] That's because many teenagers are still figuring out what they want to be or to have, so they're willing to experiment with the things they buy.

2 How do advertisers try to convince you to buy what they're selling? (b) [■] Advertisers and marketers want to get your attention and convince you that you need a product, so that you'll buy it. Brands* that try to appeal to* teenagers often use the insecurities many teenagers feel. (c) [■] They know that teenagers generally want to fit in and that they want others to think they are attractive. And because they know that teenagers are very aware of the importance of peer* groups, advertisers sometimes try to get them to trust their advice on what to have or how to look.

3 What can you do to protect yourself from marketing and advertisements like this? Think about what advertisements are trying to tell you and how they are doing it. If you could buy what they're selling, would it really make you happy? Is the product itself really appealing or does its appeal come from the models and scenery used to present it? Another thing to look out for is called 'product placement'. Advertisers and marketers try to show off their products in video games, films, on television shows or with websites that are popular with teenagers. They want young consumers to think, 'Oh, those are the shoes that I saw on TV last night!' (d) [■] Think about it the next time you are watching television and a character holds a carton of orange juice or a can of fizzy drink. Can you see the brand name? That is an example of product placement.

4 Remember, you don't have to let advertisers tell you who you are! Who you are isn't determined by what you buy or own.

demographic *a particular group of people*
brand *a type of product made by a particular company*
appeal to *to be something that people like or want*

peer *a person who belongs to the same age or social group as someone else*

8C New things from old ones

GRAMMAR Defining relative clauses

1 What does the word in bold in each sentence refer to?

1 The boy **who** is wearing the striped shirt is my brother.
  a boy
  b me
  c shirt

2 The woman **that** has the sandals and glasses is my aunt.
  a my
  b sandals
  c woman

3 Films **that** have a lot of drama are my favourite.
  a drama
  b films
  c favourite

4 I don't like food **which** is very spicy.
  a me
  b food
  c spicy

5 She likes the flowers **which** have purple and red petals the best.
  a her
  b flowers
  c petals

6 The tree **that** is in our back garden has been there for more than 100 years.
  a back garden
  b 100 years
  c tree

7 People **who** like dogs usually also like cats.
  a cats and dogs
  b like
  c people

8 Can you pass me the bag **that** is over there on the sofa?
  a bag
  b sofa
  c there

2 Complete the sentences with *who, which* or *that*. There may be more than one correct answer.

1 People _____ live in Buenos Aires call themselves *porteños*.

2 Argentina is a country _____ is famous for tango dancing.

3 A type of coffee _____ is called *cortado* is served in many cafés in Buenos Aires.

4 Many shops _____ are popular in Buenos Aires don't open until 10am.

5 People _____ like sweets might enjoy *medialunas*, which are Argentine croissants.

6 Many chefs _____ cook in Buenos Aires' more modern restaurants learned to cook in Europe.

7 Soho and Hollywood are two areas of Buenos Aires _____ have many interesting shops as well as cafés and ice cream shops.

3 Match the two parts of the sentences.

1 I don't like people
2 I like to drink water
3 The classmate
4 The dog
5 The neighbour
6 Have you seen the Degas painting
7 The painting
8 The medicine

  a who plays loud music often keeps me up at night.
  b that shows two girls sitting together is beautiful.
  c who are unkind.
  d that the museum has just bought?
  e that he needs is so expensive.
  f who lent me her book said I could keep it until our next lesson.
  g that isn't filtered.
  h that is barking is disturbing the whole street.

4 Use the prompts to write sentences with defining relative clauses. Some of the sentences do not need the relative pronoun.

Example: most of / people / I / spoke to / very friendly
Most of the people who / that I spoke to were very friendly.
OR
Most of the people I spoke to were very friendly.

1 the chair / we / bought on sale / so ugly

_____

2 he's / the teacher / gave me / advice / about / my career

_____

3 being / a chemist / a job / I / would consider

_____

4 beans / a nutrious food / have / a lot of / protein

_____

5 my father / is making / a potato recipe / he found / on the internet

_____

6 the book / is about / man / sailed / around the world / on a small boat

_____

5 Are the words in bold correct? Correct those that are incorrect.

1 I like any **food who has** chocolate in it.

_____

2 Do you want to go to the **restaurants that has** the best chef in town?

_____

3 **People which goes** to my school are the best at science.

_____

4 The **boy who stayed up** all night studying for his science exam was very tired the next day in class.

_____

5 Is being a tour guide a **jobs who pay** a lot of money?

_____

6 Talking to many people every week was very important to the **woman which wanted** to be president.

_____

7 Every **runner who finished** the race received a medal.

_____

6 Put the words in the correct order to make sentences.

1 goes / She / Bangkok / has / a / to / brother / who / school / in

_____

2 with / laughed / the / told / woman / Everyone / joke / funny / who / the

_____

3 The / that / made / soup / for / was / dinner / delicious / she

_____

4 the / I / met / our / is / girl / new / that / neighbour

_____

5 animal / type / will / An / eat / is / an / that / any / of / omnivore / food

_____

6 They / big tree / that / the / fell down during / the / removed / storm

_____

7 not / Cola / a / drink / is / I / often / which / buy

_____

8 a / uncle / She / an / who / has / is / nurse

_____

7 Complete the paragraph with *which, who, that* or – (if no pronoun is necessary). There may be more than one correct answer.

GoFundMe is a company **(1)** _____ is based in San Diego, California. Brad Damphousse and Andrew Ballester are the people **(2)** _____ started the company in 2010. GoFundMe helps people develop websites **(3)** _____ they can use to raise money for different reasons. People **(4)** _____ use GoFundMe usually need money for university, a new business or have a personal need. Many people visit GoFundMe pages because they want to give money to people **(5)** _____ need help. And these are pages **(6)** _____ can really help people! For example, a campaign **(7)** _____ was trying to help people affected by Hurricane Matthew in 2016 raised $3 million.

8 Use the prompts to write sentences with defining relative clauses that are true for you.

Example: I like apartments *that have balconies.*

1 I like to buy things _____

_____

_____

2 I like to go to restaurants _____

_____

_____

3 I like to shop in places _____

_____

_____

4 I like to talk to people _____

_____

_____

5 I visit websites _____

_____

_____

6 I have lessons _____

_____

_____

7 I know _____

_____

_____

8 I don't like _____

_____

_____

8D Our campaign to ban plastic bags in Bali

TEDTALKS

AUTHENTIC LISTENING SKILLS

1 Listen to the TED Talk extracts and complete the sentences. 🎧 86

1 Also, at the _____ Airport of Bali, one of our _____ are planning to start a plastic bag-free policy by 2016.

2 _____ handing out _____ plastic bags and bring in your own _____ bag is our _____ to change that mindset of the public.

3 Our short-term campaign, 'One Island / One Voice', is all about this. We _____ and recognize the shops and restaurants that have declared themselves a plastic bag-free zone, and we put _____ at their entrance and publish their names on social media and some important magazines on Bali. And conversely, that highlights those who do _____ the sticker.

WATCH ▶

2 Watch the TED Talk. Are the sentences true (T) or false (F)?

1 In Bali, nearly ten percent of plastic bags are recycled. _____

2 Almost all plastic bags in Bali end up in rivers or the sea. _____

3 Melati and Isabel's effort is called 'Hello Plastic Bags.' _____

4 Their parents took Melati and Isabel to visit the office of Mahatma Ghandhi. _____

5 After the visit, they decided they would stop eating for a cause. _____

6 Melati and Isabel went on a hunger strike without permission from their parents. _____

7 They have been working for almost three years now on their effort. _____

3 Choose the correct words to complete the sentences.

1 Melati and Isabel started a campaign to *help reuse / help reduce* plastic bags in Bali.

2 Their campaign *did well / did not do well*.

3 They learned after their research that there was *something / nothing* good about plastic bags.

4 They went to India to *give a talk / go on a hunger strike*.

5 They convinced their *nutritionist / teachers* to let them go on a hunger strike.

6 They did not eat from *sunrise / midday* until the sun went down every day.

7 They want the public to *stop handing out / bring their own* reusable bags when they shop.

4 Underline the things that Isabel and Melati did and do for their campaign.

1 hunger strike

2 had a business plan

3 social media

4 had a hidden agenda

5 stopped handing out plastic bags

6 remind the governor of his promise

7 check and recognize shops and restaurants that don't use plastic bags

VOCABULARY IN CONTEXT

5 Match the words with the correct paraphrased line from the talk.

1 do something about it _____

2 walk your talk _____

3 go for it _____

4 be the change _____

5 make that difference _____

a **Cause a change**. We're not telling you it's going to be easy.

b So we decided to **take action**.

c Sometimes it does get a little bit hard to **do as you say**.

d So to all the kids of this beautiful but challenging world: **act now**!

e Kids have so much energy and a desire to **live in a way that** the world needs.

6 After everything you have learned about plastic bags, what do you think about their effect on the environment? Are you thinking about making any changes in your life as a result?

8E Call to action

SPEAKING

Speaking strategies

How to persuade

Use logic:

Research shows that… ; Science has proven that… ; If… , then…

Use emotion:

Think of… ; How would you feel if… ?; My heart tells me that…

Use morals (right and wrong):

… is the right thing to do.

It's wrong to…

1 Complete each sentence with a phrase from the Speaking strategies box. Then decide if the argument is logical (L), emotional (E) or moral (M).

1 _____ smoking causes cancer. _____

2 _____ we should take care of animals. _____

3 _____ recycled more of the plastic we use, _____ less rubbish would go into the sea. _____

4 Leaving our children a healthy planet _____ . _____

5 _____ there was advertising everywhere you went? _____

6 _____ let people suffer from curable diseases. _____

7 _____ the animals that live in the sea. They get trapped in the rubbish and die. _____

8 _____ the Earth is getting warmer. _____

Listen and check your answers. 🎧 **87**

2 Complete the exchanges with the sentences (a–d) and phrases from the Speaking strategies box.

1 A _____
  B OK, but _____ testing on animals is wrong.

2 A _____
  B But _____ nuclear energy is more expensive than green energy.

3 A _____ how ugly wind turbines make the countryside look.
  B _____

4 A _____ put people in prison for life.
  B _____

a I don't care. Using renewable energy is the right thing to do.

b Well, how would you feel if they harmed someone in your family?

c Science has proven that animal testing is necessary.

d If we don't use nuclear power, then global warming will increase.

3 Think about how you would challenge the views in the sentences below. Make notes and use the Speaking strategies. Then listen to the model answers and compare them with your ideas. 🎧 **88**

1 The environment is always changing. Global warming is just a myth.

2 There is too much immigration into the country. The government should keep jobs for the local people.

_____

_____

_____

_____

4 You are going to respond to a question. Make notes on your ideas and use the Speaking strategies. Speak for 45 seconds and record yourself. Then listen to a model answer. 🎧 **89**

Some people believe that seagulls in the city are a real nuisance and something should be done about them. What do you think and why? Include examples and details in your explanation.

_____

_____

_____

WRITING A persuasive blog post

5 Read and label the persuasive blog post with the correct information (a–i).

---

(1) _____ **Community gardens would improve our city**

(2) _____ Some of the best cities in the world have community gardens! These are shared spaces in cities where people work together to grow flowers, vegetables and fruit. **(3)** _____ I saw community gardens in Taipei and in Victoria, Australia. There is also community gardening in Barcelona, London, Seattle, Ottawa, Los Angeles, Honolulu and many other great cities. Our city has no community gardens and we believe it should.

(4) _____ Research shows that community gardens bring different people together and help to create an improved sense of community.

(5) _____ Imagine you're walking through a typical urban landscape, all concrete and steel, and suddenly you see the bright colours of a garden right in the middle of the city. **(6)** _____ Wouldn't it make you feel so much better?

(7) _____ Young people in our city centre have no access to a real garden. **(8)** _____ If we allowed community gardens, children would learn more about where food really comes from, plus it would help them to appreciate nature. The gardens would also help to reduce pollution.

(9) _____ Please click here to join our campaign and get involved today!

---

a adding a call to action
b asking readers to think of an experience
c describing an emotional aspect
d explaining what would be right
e explaining what's wrong
f including a personal story
g introducing the topic
h supplying examples of success
i title

6 Read the blog post again. Then put the blogger's points in the correct order.

_____ Community gardens mean less pollution.
_____ Children learn where food comes from.
_____ Great cities have community gardens.
_____ It helps children to appreciate nature.
_____ Sense of community is improved.
_____ Community gardens bring people together.
_____ Gardens in city centres make us feel better.

7 Write a persuasive blog post supporting more independent shops in your town. Listen to the lecture and read the passage. In your blog post, summarize the points made in the the lecture and be sure to explain how they oppose specific points made in the reading passage. 🎧 90

Well-known retail chains continually open new outlets in cities and towns where they have immediate access to large populations. People want products they can trust and, more importantly, they want value for money. From supermarkets to cafés to clothing shops, we all know the familiar brands that deliver on convenience and price. Consumers know where to go for what they need and which chains can supply at low cost and still make a profit.

In principle, everybody wins except, perhaps, independent shops. These typically small shops are generally owned by one or two local people. They cannot possibly compete with the chains which are usually run by large corporations. In many cases, they fail after a couple of years and close down. While the idea of independent shops is a nice one, it is not practical. It's simply not realistic for these small shops to provide the same range of products as chains, nor to provide goods as cheaply.

Be sure to:
- Introduce your topic with a personal story.
- Mention successful examples of the change you're arguing for.
- Ask readers to think of their own experience and describe the emotional side of your proposal.
- Explain what's wrong and what would be right.
- End with a call to action that explains exactly what you think people should do.

Review

1 Match the statements.

1 The average American puts 30 kilos of clothing in the bin every year.

2 In today's big supermarkets, there are so many brands and varieties of each product, it can be hard to make a decision.

3 The toy company Mattel makes around $6 billion per year.

4 Shoe manufacturers often use leather, plastic, rubber, cotton and wood.

5 Adidas is producing athletic shoes made from plastic rubbish collected from the sea.

a There are too many options.
b They throw it away.
c They are recycling.
d They sell a lot of products.
e They use different materials.

2 Complete the sentences with the correct words.

1 Companies a_____ their products so that more people will know about them and buy them.

2 Many electronics, clothes and other items are m_____ in Chinese factories.

3 It's possible to r_____ objects in creative ways: for example, you can reuse a glass bottle and make a lamp out of it.

4 Toyota p_____ more than 10 million cars every year.

5 Coco Chanel d_____ simple, stylish clothing for women in Paris in the 1920s.

6 WalMart started as one discount department store in the 1950s and g_____ into one of the largest companies in the world, with more than 11,000 stores in 28 countries.

3 Rearrange the words to complete either the *if*-clause or the main clause (past simple).

1 often / so / buy / they / wouldn't / phones
If people didn't always want the latest and most advanced smartphone,

_____.

2 smartphone / better / them / much / makers / If / pressure / didn't / feel / so / to make

_____,

the manufacturing processes wouldn't need to change.

3 wouldn't / outdated / become / smartphones
If engineers didn't update the hardware and software,

_____.

4 test / if / prototype / the designers / didn't / a
The factory wouldn't be able to make new smartphones

_____.

5 smartphones / be / able / We / new / wouldn't / to buy

_____

if the factory didn't assemble the components.

6 wasn't / loaded / If / onto / the software / phone / the

_____,

the phone wouldn't work correctly.

4 Match the two parts of the sentences.

1 If I had enough time to study and clean my room,
2 If my classes this term weren't so challenging,
3 If I were you,
4 If we had a car,
5 If I liked vegetables,
6 If I had a degree,

a I wouldn't take too many difficult subjects.
b I could bake a cake for my friend's birthday next week.
c I could get a good job.
d I would be able to keep up with all the homework that my maths teacher gives us.
e I would order the pizza that has peppers and mushrooms on it.
f we could go to the forest which has the cycling trails.

5 Look at the list of words associated with things we buy. Use sentences with defining relative clauses to say what each thing is. Use your dictionary if necessary.

1 plastic bag _____

_____

_____

2 manufacturer _____

_____

_____

3 market _____

_____

_____

4 material _____

_____

_____

5 advertise _____

_____

_____

6 throw away _____

_____

_____

9 All in a day's work

9A Work should be fun!

VOCABULARY Jobs

1 Revision Match the words with the definitions.

1 actor	**a** works at an office; wears a suit; goes to meetings
2 artist	
3 receptionist	**b** shows people around a city or museum
4 farmer	
5 cook	**c** answers phones; sits at the front desk in an office
6 waiter/waitress	
7 businessperson	**d** uses a car, lorry, taxi or bus to do his/her job
8 photographer	
9 tour guide	**e** serves food at a restaurant
10 boss	**f** helps people learn
11 driver	**g** manages and supervises people
12 teacher	
	h works on-screen in films or television
	i takes pictures with a camera
	j makes food; works in the kitchen
	k grows food; often in a rural area
	l creates beautiful or interesting objects to look at

2 Revision Choose the correct words to complete the sentences.

1 Frida Kahlo, Michelangelo and Pablo Picasso are all famous *actors* / *artists*.

2 When you have finished your meal in a restaurant, ask the *waiter* / *teacher* for the bill.

3 Before you can enter a large office building, you usually have to check in with the *boss* / *receptionist* and show your ID.

4 Museums are always interesting, but you can learn more if you ask a *driver* / *guide* to take you round and explain the items.

5 Many towns have weekend markets where you can buy vegetables and other products from local *farmers* / *photographers*.

6 In the city centre at lunchtime, you can see many *businesspeople* / *receptionists* from local offices on their mobile phones or having lunch meetings. They never seem to stop working!

7 Often, people who work as *cooks* / *bosses* don't want to make their own meals at home.

8 People often complain that *teachers* / *drivers* get long holidays, but working with children is very tiring!

3 Match the words with the definitions.

1 cleaner _____
2 accountant _____
3 lawyer _____
4 factory worker _____
5 construction worker _____
6 salesperson _____
7 paramedic _____
8 nurse _____
9 dentist _____

a a person who builds houses

b a person who washes the floors, vacuums, takes out rubbish, etc.

c a person who works at a hospital and helps sick and injured people

d a person who drives an ambulance and responds to medical emergencies

e an office worker who is very good with numbers

f a person who helps customers and sells products in a shop

g a person who helps to put together, pack and ship products

h a highly-paid worker who represents people who are victims of crimes or who are accused of crimes

i someone whose job is to look after people's teeth

4 Listen. What is each person's job? Choose the correct answer. 🎧 91

1 a lawyer
  b secondary-school teacher
  c police officer

2 a firefighter
  b construction worker
  c nurse

3 a accountant
  b doctor
  c chief executive

4 a electronic engineer
  b software developer
  c salesperson

5 a office worker
  b construction worker
  c architect

6 a chef
  b manager
  c chief executive

5 Complete the text. Write one word in each gap.

If you're thinking about pursuing a well-paid career, you should consider going to university and maybe even getting postgraduate qualifications.

A **(1)** _____ usually spends three years at university studying law then three years in professional training.

A **(2)** _____ needs even more: five years in medical school and three to four years of professional training. If the business world is more your style, then you'll need a four-year business degree plus a master's degree (MBA) in order to become the
(3) _____ of a company.

But if a four-year university course isn't your thing, you can still become successful. For example, if you're a people person and you're good at selling, you could become a well-paid **(4)** _____. You could get a job at a big company! Or, you could attend catering college and become a **(5)** _____. You might work at a great restaurant or even start your own restaurant. Maybe you could even be a celebrity chef on TV!

A lot of people start out as a low-paid worker and move up in the company, becoming a **(6)** _____ responsible for other people. For example, you could spend a few years working in the construction industry as a **(7)** _____, gain building skills and knowledge, and eventually become the boss or start your own building company. It's the same in other industries. You could start out as a **(8)** _____ and one day open your own cleaning company.

Whatever you choose, put your heart into it and you will achieve success!

6 **Extension** Read the letter and choose the correct option to complete the sentences.

Dear Ms O'Connell,
I'm writing in response to the accounting job you posted yesterday. I am currently **(1)** _____ as an accountant at a small company and I enjoy working here.
a getting a job   **c** unemployed
b out of work   **d** employed

However, this was my first job after graduating from university and I have been here for six years. So now I am ready for a new **(2)** _____.
a internship   **c** challenge
b freedom   **d** excitement

In a small company, there is not a lot of room to grow. For this reason, I am interested in the **(3)** _____ to work in a large and growing company such as yours.
a opportunity   **c** employment
b excitement   **d** benefit

I think the experience will really help my **(4)** _____.
a adventure   **c** salary
b career   **d** application

I have attached my **(5)** _____ for your review. There, you can see the details of my work experience.
a salary   **c** apply
b employment   **d** CV

You will see that I am **(6)** _____ of four large accounts and I also manage the interns.
a full-time   **c** out of work
b in charge   **d** an expert

I think you'll find that I am a quick learner and **(7)** _____ who will always do the best job I possibly can. I am sure my manager would agree.
a an assistant   **c** a hard worker
b professional   **d** slow

I would like to meet with you as soon as possible to discuss the job further and to learn more about the salary and **(8)** _____.
a benefits   **c** danger
b adventure   **d** assistants

Please feel free to call or email. I look forward to talking with you.

Yours sincerely,
Kate Hawkins, ACA

PRONUNCIATION Question intonation

7 Listen. Does the intonation rise or fall at the end of each question? Then practise saying the questions. 🎧 92

1 rising ∧	falling ∨	**5** rising ∧	falling ∨
2 rising ∧	falling ∨	**6** rising ∧	falling ∨
3 rising ∧	falling ∨	**7** rising ∧	falling ∨
4 rising ∧	falling ∨	**8** rising ∧	falling ∨

LISTENING

8 Listen to the speakers and choose their jobs. 🎧 93

1 a fisherman
  b vet
  c marine biologist

2 a paramedic
  b doctor
  c mechanic

3 a lawyer
  b architect
  c teacher

4 a paramedic
  b factory worker
  c software developer

5 a architect
  b accountant
  c teacher

6 a chef
  b farmer
  c grocer

9 Listen to the conversation and answer the questions. 🎧 94

1 What had the young man already done by the time he was at college?
  a decided to become a nurse
  b taken online classes
  c had a few jobs

2 What position is the man applying for?
  a nurse
  b porter
  c paramedic

3 Why does this man think that this job is different from his previous ones?
  a He thinks it's a serious job.
  b He thinks it pays more money.
  c He thinks it will be a lot of fun.

4 What do porters do?
  a wash patients **c** move patients
  b feed patients

5 What word means *a kind of bed on wheels*?
  a a trolley **c** an ambulance
  b a wheelchair

6 What does the man eventually want to become?
  a a porter **c** a doctor
  b a registered nurse

7 When the woman says 'stranger things have happened,' what does she mean?
  a that she wouldn't be very surprised
  b that she thinks it's very unusual
  c that she really doesn't expect it to happen

10 Listen and answer the questions. 🎧 95

1 What would be the best title for this talk?
  a Overworked and underpaid
  b Live to work or work to live
  c Life is work and work is life
  d How to retire early

2 What does the speaker ask questions about?
  a the balance between working days and nights
  b the balance between work and life
  c the best ways to find happiness
  d the negative impact of life on work

3 Why do some people say it's OK to work as long and as hard as necessary?
  a because life is very expensive
  b because you have to earn success
  c because you shouldn't waste time
  d because a personal life isn't important

4 How would you describe a person who works 60 hours a week?
  a very lazy
  b very angry
  c very busy
  d very wealthy

5 What do you think the expression *around the clock* means?
  a working a twelve-hour day
  b from noon to midnight
  c after work
  d all day and all night

6 Which point of view does the speaker agree with?
  a the first one
  b the second one
  c neither
  d both

GRAMMAR Past perfect

11 Look at the tense of the underlined verb in each sentence. Is the sentence in the past simple (S), present perfect (P) or past perfect (PP)?

1 By the time I <u>had found</u> a job, I didn't have any money left. _____
2 I <u>did not go</u> to university straight after school; I took a gap year. _____
3 My friend <u>has had</u> a job at a bookshop since last summer. _____
4 The job market <u>had</u> already <u>become</u> worse when I returned from travelling. _____
5 My girlfriend <u>stayed</u> here and helped her grandparents after she graduated. _____
6 <u>Have</u> you <u>worked</u> in the city centre for a long time? _____
7 The company <u>had advertised</u> my job online. _____
8 My cousins and I <u>went</u> to the beach every day last summer. _____
9 I <u>hadn't seen</u> the job ad before Fay told me about it. _____

12 Read the sentences. Which action happened first (1) and which happened second (2)?

1 Before she went to university, she had been to school in her town.
go to university: _____
go to school: _____
2 I put on clean clothes after I had had a shower.
put on clothes: _____
have shower: _____
3 Before he planted the seeds, we had prepared the soil.
plant seeds: _____
prepare soil: _____
4 They had tried very hard, but they lost the game by one point.
try hard: _____
lose game: _____
5 Before they saw the film, they had read the book.
see film: _____
read book: _____
6 After she had read the online job ad, she updated her CV.
read job ad: _____
update CV: _____
7 He enjoyed his job after his manager had promoted him.
enjoy job: _____
get promotion: _____
8 She fixed the software bug after she had identified the error in the code.
fix software bug: _____
identify error: _____

13 Listen to the job interview. Then complete the sentences using the past perfect. 🎧 96

1 What had Martina done as chef at the Japanese restaurant?
As chef, she _____ the menus and _____ the food.
2 What had Martina done at the Greek restaurant?
She _____ a cook and _____ the main dishes.
3 What had Martina done at her aunt's restaurant?
She _____ the tables and _____ food to the customers.
4 What had Martina learned at school?
She _____ the basics of working in a restaurant kitchen as well as the usual school subjects.
5 What had Martina done at home?
She _____ her parents cook meals at home.

14 Correct the mistakes with the past perfect in the sentences.

1 Before you text your friend, had you receive your teacher's email?
_____
2 After the teacher had give them the essay, they go to the library to research the topic.
_____
3 Before you had ate dinner, you had finish your homework.
_____
4 Before the meeting, the manager prepare a schedule that work for everyone.
_____
5 Before we had cooked lunch, we had buy all the ingredients.
_____
6 He creates a fan website for his favourite band after he had saw a fan site for another band.
_____
7 Had you meet before I had introduce you yesterday?
_____
8 Hadn't you do any preparation before you go to the interview?
_____

9B What do you want to be when you grow up?

VOCABULARY BUILDING Dependent prepositions

1 Match the two parts of the sentences.

1 Scientists and engineers
2 Zaro Bates grows food on an urban farm
3 Ideas taken from computer science and chemistry
4 One important source of green energy
5 Wind energy and clean cars

a are often used in clean car technology.
b is power from sea waves.
c work together on the development of clean cars.
d are two types of exciting, green technology.
e and sells it at a community food stand.

READING

2 Read the text and choose the correct answer to the questions.

1 The author uses the phrase *play a big role* in paragraph 1 to mean

   a be a source of green energy.
   b be on stage.
   c be important.
   d be worth a lot of money.

2 The word *green* in paragraph 1 means

   a not natural.
   b not harmful to the environment.
   c relating to the wind and sea.
   d natural.

3 What is the author's purpose?

   a to help people find jobs
   b to help sell electric cars
   c to give examples of green jobs
   d to give an opinion on the best jobs

4 Which of the following statements about the urban farm is not true?

   a The farm produces honey.
   b There are chickens at the farm.
   c Some of the food goes to food banks.
   d The farm produces a lot of food.

5 The meaning of the word *generate* in paragraph 5 is similar to

   a produce.   c power.
   b reduce.   d turn on.

6 According to paragraph 5, what does a wave farm produce?

   a electricity   c technology
   b wind   d clean fuel

3 Match the jobs with the descriptions.

1 urban farmer
2 software developer
3 production manager
4 chemical engineer
5 materials scientist

a studies materials and how to use them
b plans the activities needed to manufacture something
c works on making batteries better
d grows enough food to sell in a city
e works with computers in cars

4 Choose the correct option to complete the sentences.

1 Chemical and electrical _____ work together to develop clean car technology.

   a vehicles
   b engineers
   c manufacture
   d managers

2 Software developers use ideas _____ computer science to create computers for clean cars.

   a belong to
   b made from
   c taken from
   d added to

3 Wave energy will be an important source of _____ energy in the future.

   a solar
   b renewable
   c power
   d technology

4 Working on clean cars, urban farms and wave energy are three types of _____ jobs that we can look forward to in the future.

   a green
   b engineering
   c electrical
   d renewable

5 Answer the questions about the article with your own ideas.

1 What kind of green job would you like to know more about?

   _____
   _____

2 Do you know anyone who works in a green job? What does he or she do?

   _____
   _____

3 Do you think green jobs are important? Why? / Why not?

   _____
   _____

Green jobs of the future

1 🎧 **97** You've heard about green energy, green buildings and green products. The future is green and green jobs will play a big role in that future. Is there a green job in your future? Have you thought about what you'd like to do when you're ready to start working? If you have, then you might want to learn more about green jobs like these.

Clean cars

2 People with different skills work on developing electric, or clean, vehicles from the first designs to manufacturing a car. These projects require people with backgrounds in science, engineering, maths, computers, business and manufacturing.

- Chemical engineers bring ideas from chemistry and use them to design or improve equipment. An important part of their work is developing and improving battery designs.

- Materials scientists study what materials, such as aluminium, are being used in electric cars and their batteries. They examine what materials are made of in order to improve them or create new ones. For example, electric cars need to be lightweight, so a materials scientist needs to identify strong and lightweight materials to use.

- Electrical engineers design, develop and test the electrical parts of the vehicle. They design the system that makes it possible for a petrol engine and a battery to work together.

- Software developers use their knowledge of maths and computers to design software that controls the car engine. Electric and hybrid cars have built-in computers that control the engine and battery systems depending on the situation.

- Production managers plan and organize the people, equipment and parts needed to build and assemble vehicles and vehicle parts.

Urban farming

3 Zaro Bates runs a farm on Staten Island in New York City. The farm is between two large apartment buildings, but it's not a garden. At 4,500 square feet (465 square metres), it is a commercial farm that produces vegetables and other products for sale. In fact, one day a week from spring to autumn, Zaro sells produce* at the apartments.

4 What does Bates grow on the urban farm? About 50 different kinds of produce including vegetables and herbs. The farm even produces honey. In fact, Bates is able to grow so much food that she donates some of it to food banks.

Wave energy

5 Ocean waves are a powerful source of renewable energy. Wave energy is green and it can be used in ways that do not harm sea life. A wave power 'farm' is a number of machines that generate electricity from power created by the waves. One type of wave power farm operates on the energy that's created when a float on a large buoy* moves with the waves in the sea. The Aguçadoura Wave Farm, the world's first, is off the coast of northern Portugal.

6 Wave energy is a new technology, but it holds great promise. Engineers, managers and scientists will be the wave 'farmers' of the future. Could there be a wave in your future?

produce *vegetables, fruit, herbs*
buoy *a floating object used to mark an area in water*

9C She said it wasn't just about the money

GRAMMAR Reported speech

1 Listen and complete the sentences. 🎧 98

1 She told her sons it _____ time for dinner.

2 Lee _____ if I had been to Cambodia.

3 I told Lee _____ to Cambodia when I was at secondary school.

4 She _____ *Harry Potter and the Philospher's Stone* was her favourite book.

5 Sophie _____ Buenos Aires was her favourite city.

6 Kanata said _____ to the Sydney Opera House.

7 He _____ he was worried he would fail the exam because he forgot to revise.

8 My father _____ if I wanted some bread with my soup.

2 Choose the correct reported speech option for each example of direct speech.

1 My grandmother: 'Always work smarter, not harder.'

  a My grandmother said to always work smarter, not harder.

  b My grandmother will say to always work smarter, not harder.

2 Martin: 'I studied all week for the exam and know I will get a good mark.'

  a Martin said he could be studying all week for the exam and knows he'd get a good mark.

  b Martin said he'd studied all week for the exam and knew he'd get a good mark.

3 My grandfather: 'You've made me proud.'

  a My grandfather told me I had made him proud.

  b My grandfather told me I had him proud.

4 Me: 'Is Jane Goodall an important scientist?'

  a I ask if Jane Goodall is an important scientist.

  b I asked if Jane Goodall was an important scientist.

5 My sister: 'I rode my bike to school every day last year.'

  a My sister said me she rode her bike to school every day last year.

  b My sister told me she had ridden her bike to school every day last year.

6 My uncle: 'The train won't be on time.'

  a My uncle said the train wouldn't be on time.

  b My uncle said me the train can't be on time.

7 My friends Carlos and Luis: 'We can't come to your party this weekend.'

  a Carlos and Luis said they couldn't come to my party this weekend.

  b Carlos and Luis said they could come to my party this weekend.

8 Eun: 'I can look after your pets while you're on holiday.'

  a Eun told me she could look after my pets while I was on holiday.

  b Eun told me she will look after my pets while I was on holiday.

3 Choose the correct words to complete the reported speech.

1 The salesman said, 'You will have to pay more money for the car you want.'

  He said that I *would / could* have to pay more money for the car I wanted.

2 She said, 'I'm travelling to Chile for work.'

  She *told that / told me that* she *was travelling / travelled* to Chile for work.

3 'I visited my grandmother every week,' she told her friend.

  She / You told her friend that she *had visited / wouldn't visit* her grandmother every week.

4 My friend asked, 'Do you want to go cycling tomorrow?'

  He asked if I wanted to go cycling *the next day / tomorrow*.

5 He asked, 'What are you writing?'

  He *said / asked* me what I *was writing / had written*.

6 Dad said, 'Mei, open our windows to let some cooler air in.'

  Dad *told Mei to / told to Mei* open *our / their* windows to let some cooler air in.

7 Sejal said, 'I've been to Majorca for a holiday.'

  Sejal told me *she'd been / she went* to Majorca for a holiday.

8 I said, 'Sejal, I went to Majorca last year.'

  I told Sejal *I'd been / I had been going to* Majorca the year before.

9 Our English teacher said, 'You can finish the essay in class.'

  Our English teacher *told us / told* that we *could / would* finish the essay in class.

4 Put the words in the correct order to make sentences.

1 couldn't / He / them / eat / told / the / salad / they

_____.

2 was / He / some / he / going / to / said / eggs / buy

_____.

3 that / late / She / she / could / tell / our / I'd / be / said / teacher

_____.

4 He / travel / planning / told / he / me / to / to / was / Asia

_____.

5 worked / they / me / project / told / They / on / that

_____.

6 She / the / she / previous / watched / the / news / said / night / had

_____.

7 couldn't / parents / They / eat / dinner / with / they / their / said

_____.

8 asked / would / he / him / if / help / I

_____.

5 Put the words or phrases in the table to show the tense changes from direct speech to reported speech. Use one word or phrase twice.

could / couldn't	past perfect	present continuous
past simple	past simple	will / won't

Direct speech	Reported speech
present simple	
	past continuous
	past simple / past perfect
present perfect	
	would / wouldn't
can / can't	

6 Are the words in bold correct? Correct those that are incorrect.

1 He **told he** couldn't lend me any money.

_____

2 She **asked me** not to go to the beach without her.

_____

3 He said one of the best art museums in the country **was** in our city.

_____

4 Marta said **she'd** look it up online.

_____

7 Listen to the radio report. Then rewrite the sentences as reported speech. 🎧 99

1 The reporter said, 'It's 10pm on a cool Saturday in Los Angeles.'

_____

2 The reporter said, 'The van will be open for the next few hours…'

_____

3 The reporter said, 'Kogi BBQ has been popular since 2008…'

_____

4 The reporter said, '…two friends had the idea of serving Korean barbecue together with Mexican tacos…'

_____

5 The reporter said, 'Many think it's good enough to queue for!'

_____

8 Choose the correct words to complete the sentences.

1 She told me she *gave* / *given* people legal advice and information. She's a *lawyer* / *nurse*.

2 He said he *was trained* / *won't trained* to help people who are sick or injured, and he received more training than a nurse. He's a *chef* / *doctor*.

3 She said she *that was helping* / *was going to help* teenagers learn. She will be a *secondary-school teacher* / *dentist*.

4 They *told us* / *told* they designed devices like mp3 players and smartphones. They're *accountants* / *electronic engineers*.

5 He said he *can* / *couldn't* provide care for people's teeth and mouths. He's not a *dentist* / *teacher*.

6 She told us she *designed* / *will design* computer programs. She's *an architect* / *a software developer*.

7 He told me he *won't* / *could* prepare financial information. He's an *architect* / *accountant*.

8 They said they *prepared and cooked* / *going to prepare and cook* food as a job. They're *chefs* / *lawyers*.

9 Rewrite the sentences as reported speech.

1 John said, 'I can't print my project from that computer.'

_____

2 She said, 'I lived in Copenhagen until I was at secondary school.'

_____

3 She said, 'Yesterday I walked from our school to the library.'

_____

4 My parents said, 'We turned the lights on.'

_____

5 He said, 'I can't take the history exam today.'

_____

9D The surprising thing I learned sailing solo around the world

TEDTALKS

AUTHENTIC LISTENING SKILLS

1 Listen to the TED Talk extract and underline the weak forms with the schwa sound. 🎧 **100**

I will never forget the excitement as we closed the coast. I will never forget the feeling of adventure as I climbed on board the boat and stared into her tiny cabin for the first time. But the most amazing feeling was the feeling of freedom, the feeling that I felt when we hoisted her sails.

WATCH ▷

2 Watch the TED Talk and put the events in the correct order.

_____ She begins her apprenticeship in sailing.

_____ She sits in a design meeting designing a boat for her to travel alone around the world.

_____ Dame Ellen MacArthur sails for the first time.

_____ She misses an iceberg by twenty feet.

_____ She finishes in second place.

_____ She saves her school dinner money change for eight years.

3 Are the sentences true (T) or false (F)?

1 When Ellen was a child, she often dreamed of sailing. _____

2 During a race, her boat blew on its side in the Southern Ocean. _____

3 She was at sea for three years for the race. _____

4 She enjoyed the race so much, she decided to do another race and sail around the world. _____

5 She says that a boat is an entire world and what you take is all you have. _____

6 Sailing on a boat helped Ellen to understand that there is an end to things – what we have is all we have. _____

4 Choose the correct answer to the questions.

1 What is the speaker mainly discussing?

a how sailing is the best hobby

b how she went from sailing to what she does now

c why coal is limited and important

2 What does the speaker do now?

a She runs an organization.

b She sails in races.

c She speaks about sailing.

3 Why does the speaker mention the photo of a coal-fired power station?

a to describe how coal is an important part of energy

b to talk about the coal industry

c to connect the photo to her great-grandfather

4 What does the speaker want to do with the things people use?

a She wants to use up materials.

b She wants to think of ways to reuse things.

c She wants to collect the things people use.

5 What can be inferred about the Ellen MacArthur Foundation?

a It helps build an economy that can help the future.

b It helps young people live their dream of sailing.

c It helps old people understand technology.

6 Why does the speaker mention her great-grandfather?

a to explain how old he is

b to explain how there were only 25 cars during his time

c to explain how much the world has changed

VOCABULARY IN CONTEXT

5 Match the words with the correct paraphrased line from the talk.

1 focus on

2 global

3 use up

4 freedom

5 tough

6 curiosity

a The most amazing feeling was the feeling of having **the right to do what I want**.

b Just like in my dreams, there were amazing parts and **difficult** parts.

c Our **world** economy is no different.

d And it made me make a decision that I never thought I would make: to leave solo sailing to **look closely at** the greatest challenge I'd ever seen.

e And my **desire to know more** led me to some extraordinary places.

f If we could build an economy that would use things rather than **take all of something**, we could make a future that works in the long term.

9E What does a UX designer do?

SPEAKING

1 Put the words in the correct order to make sentences and questions.

1 nurses / do / much / earn / How

_____?

2 do / What / consultant / an / does / image

_____?

3 been / architecture / I've / in / interested / always

_____.

4 gamers / do / work / Where / professional

_____?

5 paid / teachers / Are / well

_____?

6 One / history / subjects / of / favourite / is / my

_____.

7 need / What / skills / do / salespeople

_____?

2 Look at the questions and decide if the intonation rises (R) or falls (F) at the end of the question. Then listen and check your answers. 🔊 101

1 Do you work every day? _____
2 Have you ever had a part-time job? _____
3 How many hours do nurses work? _____
4 Which company do you work for? _____
5 How much training do professional gamers do? _____
6 What qualifications do teachers need? _____
7 Would you like to be a firefighter? _____
8 Are you going to get promoted? _____

3 Match the two parts of the sentences.

1 What does an online reputation manager	**a** work?
2 So, where do online reputation managers	**b** like singing.
3 I	**c** need?
4 I love	**d** social media.
5 So, what skills do these managers	**e** do?

4 Complete the conversation with the sentences and questions from Exercise 3.

A Everyone's talking about careers, but I don't know what I want to do when I'm older.

B I know. My dad said I needed to make some decisions, but **(1)** _____ and he doesn't think music is a proper career.

A So, what have you said to him?

B Well, **(2)** _____ and there's more work in that field. One new job that sounds interesting is called an online reputation manager.

A I've never heard of that before! **(3)** _____

B Well, they deal with complaints and problems on social media before they become big issues.

A Oh, OK, that sounds cool. **(4)** _____

B Usually for big companies, but it could be for bands and singers too. That's what I'd be interested in doing.

A That sounds cool! **(5)** _____
_____

B Well, online complaints can cause companies huge problems, so you have to be quick to respond to things, have great people skills and be able to communicate clearly on social media, which is great for me.

A I might have to think about a new job too. I love IT. Maybe I should look at designing social media apps or something.

B Yeah, go for it. I think there's a job out there for everyone.

5 Read the question and make some notes on your ideas for your response. Speak for about two minutes and record yourself. Then listen to the model answer and compare your ideas. 🔊 102

What kind of job would you like to have in the future?

_____
_____
_____
_____
_____
_____
_____
_____
_____
_____
_____

WRITING   A formal email

6 Read the email. Answer the questions with these words or phrases. There are two that you don't need.

a journalist	a travel writer	Alvaro Costa
formal	Ms Dixon	no
Piero Costa	yes	

Dear Ms Dixon,

My uncle, Piero Costa, gave me your name and said that you can answer some of my questions about travel writing. Thank you for taking the time to read my email. I'm in year 13 at Heaton Grammar School in Cardiff. I'm very interested in both travel and writing, and I would like to learn more about becoming a travel writer.

I have a few questions:

1 I'm not sure what subject to take. Could you tell me whether it's better to study journalism or English at university?
2 I have already written some travel writing articles, but I don't know where to send them. Do you know if there's a magazine or website that might publish them?
3 I'm trying to read as much travel writing as I can. I'd like to know who your favourite travel writers are.

Thank you again for agreeing to answer my questions. I look forward to hearing from you.

Yours sincerely,
Alvaro Costa

1 Who has information about travel writing?

_____

2 Who is a student?

_____

3 What does Alvaro want to become?

_____

4 Has Alvaro written any travel writing pieces?

_____

5 Does he say who his favourite travel writers are?

_____

6 What is the tone of the email?

_____

7 Choose the best option to complete the formal email.

Dear Mr Miller,

My teacher, Mr Benevides, has given me your name. He said that you can answer some of my questions about web design. **(1)** _____ I'm in my final year at the Oakvale High School in Singapore. I'm very interested in web design and development, and **(2)** _____

I have some questions for you:

1 **(3)** _____ Could you tell me about an average day in your job? Do you have to go to a lot of meetings?
2 I already help some of my family members with their websites and I think I could start my own business. **(4)** _____
3 I'd like to take some online courses on coding. **(5)** _____

Many thanks for taking the time to answer my questions.
(6) _____

Yours sincerely,
Junsu Chang

1 a Thank you so much for this opportunity.
  b I don't know any web developers, so thanks.

2 a I really want you to tell me about being a web developer.
  b I would like to learn more about being a web developer.

3 a I'd like to know what a typical day is like for a web developer.
  b Anyway, what's a typical day like for most web developers?

4 a So, is it better to work for a big company or to become self-employed?
  b Do you know if it's better to work for a big company or to be self-employed?

5 a Could you tell me which courses you recommend?
  b What courses do you recommend in coding?

6 a Please write back soon, Mr Miller!
  b I look forward to hearing from you.

8 Now write a formal email of your own. Choose one of the careers and follow the steps.

- police officer
- advertising executive
- make-up artist
- marketing assistant

1 Use polite and formal language.
2 Address your email to Mr Noguchi.
3 Say you got his name from your teacher, Ms Powell.
4 Thank him for the opportunity.
5 Give him some information about yourself.
6 Ask him at least three indirect questions.
7 Thank him again and request a reply.
8 Sign off appropriately.

Review

① Choose the correct words to complete the sentences.

1 To apply for a job as a salesperson, you should talk to the *store manager* / *chef*.
2 The *lawyers* / *paramedics* are usually called when there is a medical emergency.
3 After a big office party, the office *cleaners* / *architects* may have a lot of extra work to do.
4 In order to become a *dentist* / *factory worker*, you must complete several years at university.
5 *Office workers* / *Firefighters* have a difficult and dangerous job protecting people and their homes and businesses, as well as our forests.
6 In order to become an *accountant* / *executive*, you need to be good at maths and keeping records.

② Complete the sentences with the correct words.

1 One thing an e_____ e_____ might do is design and test the computer-based parts of a car.
2 The c_____ e_____ is the most senior and usually the highest-paid person in a company.
3 A p_____ o_____ has a very important job protecting the community from crime.
4 We pay a lot of money for our computers, mobile phones and designer clothes, but the f_____ w_____ who make them often don't earn very much money at all.
5 At the hospital, we depend on d_____ to explain our condition and give us advice, but it's the n_____ who take care of us.
6 You always know when f_____ are on the way because of the loud sirens and bright flashing lights on their long, red vehicles.

③ Look at the dates and events in Sheryl Sandberg's life. Then complete the sentences using the past perfect form of the verbs.

1969	born in Washington, DC
1991	BA in economics from Harvard
1992	Research Assistant at the World Bank
1995	MBA from Harvard Business School
1996	Chief of Staff at US Department of Treasury
2001	a vice president at Google
2008	Chief Operating Officer at Facebook
2012	became first woman on Facebook's Board of Directors

be	complete (x2)	graduate	work (x2)

Sheryl Sandberg is the chief operating officer at Facebook.

1 She attended Harvard University after she _____ from high school.
2 She worked at the World Bank after she _____ her studies at Harvard.
3 She went back to Harvard for her MBA after she _____ at the World Bank.
4 Before she worked at the US Department of Treasury, she _____ her MBA.
5 She _____ a vice president at Google for seven years before she got her current job at Facebook.
6 She became the first woman on the Facebook board of directors after she _____ as chief operating officer of Facebook for four years.

④ Complete the sentences with the past simple or past perfect form of the verbs in brackets.

1 He told me he _____ (enjoy; past perfect) his internship at the museum.
2 She said that in ancient Japan, farmers _____ rice and _____ (grow, sell; past simple) it.
3 Kwan told me he _____ (find; past perfect) some good places to eat near his hotel.
4 She told me she _____ (eat; past simple) lunch with her colleagues before the meeting.
5 He said he _____ (want; past simple) to find a new job.
6 She said she _____ (decide; past perfect) to study English.

⑤ Choose the correct answer for each question.

1 Do you think he'll be a great dancer?
   a Well, his teachers told him that if he practised more, he could be a great dancer.
   b Yes! His teachers are telling him that if he'd practised more, he would be a great dancer.

2 Is your teacher famous?
   a Yes, he told that he's on a winning Olympic football team in the 1990s.
   b Yes, he said that he'd been on a winning Olympic football team in the 1990s.

3 Did you win the award?
   a No, my teacher told me I didn't win it.
   b Yes! My teacher had told me I was winning it.

4 Do you know where Maria and Pedro lived when they were children?
   a They told me they could live in Bogotá when they were children.
   b Their mother said they'd lived in Bogotá until they were teenagers.

10 Remote control

10A Inventions: past, present, future

VOCABULARY Technology

1 Revision Complete the sentences with the correct words.

camera	machine	printer	programme
software	texts	tablet	video games

1 A computer is a _____ that performs many functions, including word processing, counting and storing information.

2 A _____ is like a computer, but it's smaller and has a keyboard on the screen.

3 Most mobile phones have a pretty good _____ for taking and posting photos.

4 For many people, playing _____ is a fun and challenging activity that uses several skills.

5 If you don't have access to a _____, you can send your essay to your teacher in an email.

6 I don't like talking on the phone. I usually communicate by sending _____.

7 If you know how to _____ computers, you could create _____ for a big company like Apple or Microsoft.

2 Match the words with the definitions.

1	research	**a**	an object that helps you do a job
2	equipment	**b**	all of the things that are used to do something
3	process		
4	tool	**c**	improvement that is made over time
5	invention		
6	progress	**d**	steps that you take to do something
7	control	**e**	to make something or someone do what you want
8	digital		
		f	to find out information about something
		g	a new object that someone creates
		h	storing sound or images as electronic signals

3 Choose the correct option to complete the sentences.

1 You need a lot of _____ to go camping, such as a torch, a tent and food.

   a inventions   **b** equipment   **c** process

2 Today we have powerful electric machines to do our work for us, but more than a thousand years ago, people were constructing houses and huge buildings of stone using only very simple _____.

   a research   **b** tools   **c** developments

3 These days, almost everything is digital. Instead of going to a shop to buy a CD, getting new music is now a simple _____ of going to a website or using an app and downloading files.

   a technology   **b** progress   **c** process

4 Did you know that there are some new video games that you can _____ with your brain by wearing a special device on your head?

   a control   **b** research   **c** process

5 Several companies are working on the _____ of the flying car. Some have succeeded, but it will be years before many people will be able to buy and use them.

   a equipment   **b** progress   **c** development

6 The many important _____ that were developed during the Industrial Revolution, such as the steam engine and the locomotive train, quickly and dramatically changed Europe's cities.

   a technology   **b** inventions   **c** developments

4 Read the text about tiny robots. Are the sentences (1–8) true (T), false (F) or is the information not given (NG)?

TINY ROBOTS

Since the invention of the first digital and programmable robot in 1954, robot technology has made incredible progress. Robots are now used in many different places, including factories, hospitals and the military. Robotic equipment is used for underwater research and space exploration. Robots are sent into buildings and other places that are too dangerous for people to enter.

When we think of robots, we often think of large machines – sometimes we imagine human-like machines that have a face and talk. But an interesting new development is the field of micro- and nano-robotics.

Across the globe, scientists are making and testing very tiny robots. They hope these robots will be able to go into the human body and perform tasks, such as delivering medicine to a specific area, removing a small object that was swallowed, performing surgery or making tiny repairs. They are controlled wirelessly and remotely from outside the body, but scientists hope one day to create robots that can be programmed to work independently or through a process of working together with other tiny robots.

Some people fear that their jobs will be replaced by robots, but robots could actually save their lives one day. Tiny robots could become one of the most important tools in hospitals of the future!

1 Robots have replaced around 40% of human jobs since the 1950s. _____

2 Robots are used to explore the oceans and outer space. _____

3 Very tiny robots are a standard part of most hospital equipment today. _____

4 Scientists will use a kind of remote control to move the robots inside the patient's body. _____

5 Micro- and nano-robots will be an important tool for doctors to use in the future. _____

6 Robots can do many jobs people can't do. _____

7 The first micro-robot was invented in 1954. _____

8 A lab in Japan is testing micro-robot technology to help people with stomach problems. _____

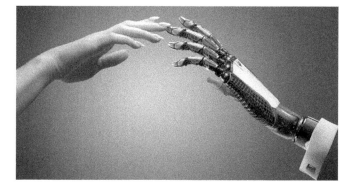

5 Extension Choose the correct words to complete the sentences.

1 After you download the software, you need to *install / produce* it on your computer.

2 The *energy / electric* that powers a mobile phone comes from a battery.

3 Scientists send robots to *engineer / explore* extremely deep areas of the ocean in the hope that they will *install / discover* something new and interesting.

4 In the future, I hope we can use *green technology / spacecraft* to reduce pollution.

5 The Swedish tech company King *produces / partners with* many popular game apps for computers and phones.

6 Some robots have been *discovered / engineered* to work independently, without a person there to control them.

7 Some mobile phone companies *partner with / explore* specific service providers to offer special deals.

6 Extension Complete the texts with the correct words and phrases.

design	discovered	electric
energy	engineer	explore
green technology	install	invention
partnering with	producing	spacecraft

1 3D printers are a useful _____. People can _____ a 3D digital model of an object and then 'print' it using materials like plastic, creating a solid object.

2 Cassini-Huygens is a robotic _____ that NASA sent to _____ Saturn in 1997. It arrived in 2004. Through Cassini, scientists _____ seven new moons orbiting Saturn and that one of the moons, Enceladus, may be able to support life.

3 With climate change as a growing problem, _____ is becoming more and more important. Many companies are researching and developing ways to use alternative _____, like solar and wind. Tesla Motors, a company famous for _____ very modern, but very expensive, _____ cars, is _____ another company, Panasonic, to _____ a new kind of solar tile that people can _____ on the roof of their house and get their electricity from the sun.

PRONUNCIATION Stress in passive verbs

7 Listen and underline the passive verb phrases. Then practise saying the sentences. 🎧 **103**

1 Electronic money is stored in Kenyans' mobile phones.
2 Birds were used by the Roman army to send messages.
3 The technology was developed by scientists in Germany.
4 The first phone call was made by Alexander Graham Bell.
5 AI, or artificial intelligence, is found in most smartphones.
6 Sometimes new technologies are invented by accident.
7 The car was driven by an intelligent computer.
8 The iPhone was launched by Apple in 2007.

LISTENING

8 Listen to the speakers. Which technology are they describing? Choose your answers from the options (a–f). 🎧 **104**

a smartphone	d wireless printer
b robotic worker	e artificial intelligence
c driverless car	f electronic money

1 _____   4 _____
2 _____   5 _____
3 _____   6 _____

9 Listen and match the products with the descriptions. 🎧 **105**

1 ilet 4	a has a 17.3 inch screen
2 Optimum 3.0	b the woman owns this laptop
3 Vertex	c the smallest laptop
4 Optimum 5.0	d has the longest lasting battery
5 Plintar	e has two USB ports

a USB port

10 Listen to the conversation and choose the sentence that describes how the girl's grandmother feels about new technology. 🎧 **106**

a She thinks it's too confusing.
b She thinks it's dangerous.
c She's not interested in it.
d She's interested, but too busy.

landline

11 Listen to the conversation again and answer the questions. 🎧 **106**

1 What does the girl find inspiring about her grandmother?
   a her kindness and generosity
   b her active lifestyle
   c her technical abilities
   d her independence

2 What problem does the girl have?
   a understanding her grandmother's life
   b getting her grandmother to respond to email
   c convincing her grandmother to get a phone
   d communicating with her grandmother

3 Why is it difficult for the girl to stay in touch with her grandmother?
   a Her grandmother doesn't like Facebook.
   b Her grandmother only has a landline phone.
   c Her grandmother rarely turns on her computer.
   d Her grandmother never checks her voicemail.

4 What does the granddaughter imply when she says: 'She was given a laptop for her birthday, but she has never learned how to use it. I don't think she's ever even turned it on.'
   a The grandmother asked for the laptop, but then changed her mind.
   b The grandmother doesn't have the time to learn how to use it.
   c The grandmother has no interest in adopting modern technology.
   d The grandmother tried to learn how to use it, but it was too difficult.

5 What does the boy suggest the girl might do?
   a teach her grandmother some technical skills
   b try to understand her grandmother's thinking
   c ask her grandmother for the new laptop
   d explain why young people do what they do

6 What does the grandmother see happening in the world?
   a people becoming less and less interested in learning
   b technology having both positive and negative effects
   c visiting people becoming more and more difficult
   d people more focused on their phones than each other

GRAMMAR The passive

12 Choose the correct verb form to complete the sentences.

1 Almost all of the 18 million smartphone users in Spain report that they *using / are used / use* apps every day.
2 A 'Great Canadian Apps' section was created in the iTunes app store because so many apps *are developed / is developed / develop* in Canada.
3 A 1% tax on smartphone users in France could fund organizations that *are created / create / creating* digital content in French.
4 Nearly 25% of smartphone users in the UK said they *being / been / are* addicted to their phones.
5 In India, it *reports / reported / was reported* that men use their smartphones mostly for apps and browsing the web, and women use their smartphones mostly for social media and messaging.
6 In China, more than 25% of the 246 million smartphone users regularly *using / use / is used* more than 21 apps on their phones.
7 Smartphones *owned / was owned / are owned* by over 80% of the population in South Korea.

13 Complete the sentences with the correct passive form of the verbs in brackets.

1 More than 650,000 books _____ (publish, past simple) in the United States in 2015.
2 In the last year, print books _____ (read, past simple) by 75% of people aged 16–29.
3 E-books _____ (purchase, past simple) by 5% of adults who purchased a book last year.
4 Print books _____ (read, present simple) by 90% of people.
5 E-books _____ (buy, present simple) by fewer than 10% of readers.
6 Almost 205,000 e-books _____ (buy, past simple) in 2015, nearly 30,000 fewer than in 2014.
7 Books that _____ (price, present simple) under £4.00 sell better than books at any other price.
8 Sales of e-books are dropping, perhaps because more than 50,000 e-books _____ (create, present simple) each month.

14 Complete the sentences and questions with the correct passive form of these verbs. There may be more than one correct answer.

| cause | earn | link | receive | (not) respond |
| send | spend | use | write | |

1 **A** When _____ the first text message _____?
   B The first text message _____ in 1992. It happened in the UK.

2 **A** How much money _____ by mobile phone companies from text messages each year?
   B Mobile phone companies earn $60–$70 billion each year from text messages.

3 **A** When _____ most text messages _____?
   B Most text messages _____ between 10:30 and 11:00pm.

4 **A** How many text messages _____ to?
   B Only 2% of text messages _____ to. That means 98% of text messages *are* responded to! Did you know that only 20% of emails are answered?

5 **A** How many car accidents _____ to texting every year?
   B More than 200,000 car accidents _____ by texting.

15 Change the sentences from active to passive or from passive to active.

1 Print books are preferred by 62% of 16- to 24-year-olds in the UK.
   _____
   _____

2 In the past, books were chained to the shelves in libraries in order to stop them from being stolen.
   _____
   _____

3 The most expensive book ever purchased, Leonardo Da Vinci's *Codex Leicester*, was bought by Bill Gates for $30.8 million.
   _____
   _____

4 92% of US college students prefer print books over digital books.
   _____
   _____

5 People in Iceland read more books per capita than in any other country.
   _____
   _____

6 Nearly half of all magazines are bought on Friday, Saturday and Sunday.
   _____
   _____

7 In 1949, a Spanish teacher patented the first electronic book because she wanted to reduce the number of books her students had to carry.
   _____
   _____

10B Can tech teach us?

VOCABULARY BUILDING Word families

1 Complete the sentences with the correct form of the words in brackets.

1 Bees, and the work they do, helped to inspire the _____ (develop) of small flying robots called 'RoboBees.'

2 Robert Wood is a professor of _____ (engineer), as well as a National Geographic Explorer.

3 Some scientists believe that RoboBees will help with the _____ (produce) of crops in the future.

4 The development of RoboBees is an important _____ (achieve).

5 The _____ (develop) of the RoboBees are a team of scientists and engineers.

6 The failure of the project was a huge _____ (disappoint) to the team.

7 People who are good at maths in school often go on to become high _____ (achieve) in the world of science and engineering.

8 When developing new technologies, engineers are constantly thinking about where they can make _____ (improve) to designs.

READING

2 Read the article about RoboBees. Choose the TWO details that are not mentioned by the author.

a RoboBees have very thin wings that flap 120 times per second.

b Portable sources of power for RoboBees must still be developed.

c RoboBees might be used to pollinate a field of crops.

d RoboBees still have to learn to communicate with each other while working.

e RoboBees can take off and hang in the air.

3 Match the information (a–e) with the paragraphs (1–4). You may use the numbers more than once.

a how RoboBees are similar to real bees _____

b possible future use for RoboBees _____

c RoboBees are only part of the answer _____

d bee populations are dropping _____

e the work of a National Geographic Explorer _____

4 Complete the summary using the passive form of the verbs in brackets.

RoboBees **(1)** _____ (develop) at the Microrobotics Lab at Harvard University by Dr Robert Wood and his team. The RoboBees **(2)** _____ (design) like real bees. Tasks can **(3)** _____ (perform) by these robotic insects. For example, crops could **(4)** _____ (pollinate) by these tiny robots if there were not enough real bees to do the work. Robotic bees **(5)** _____ (not expect) to replace real bees. However, they are one example of how problems can **(6)** _____ (solve) by new technology.

5 Read the part of the article comparing RoboBees and honeybees. Choose the correct words to complete the sentences.

1 Wingspan is the length from the tip of one *wing* / *antennae* to the tip of the other.

2 The *RoboBee* / *honeybee* has a larger wingspan.

3 The honeybee's wings beat more than 200 times *per second* / *per minute*.

4 The *RoboBee* / *honeybee* is heavier.

5 The RoboBee has a *shorter* / *longer* wingspan.

Flight of the RoboBees

1 🎧 **107** It's a bee! It's a robot! It's a RoboBee! A *what?* A RoboBee is a flying robot that's roughly the size of a bee or small flying insect. Like real bees, RoboBees can rise from a surface and hang in midair. They can be programmed to do tasks. They're small enough to go places real bees go and do the work of real bees.

2 The RoboBee was developed by electrical engineering professor and roboticist Robert Wood and his team at the Microrobotics Lab at Harvard University. Wood, who is also a National Geographic Explorer, is concerned about the fact that bee colonies all over the world are disappearing and bee populations are dropping dangerously. Why does that matter? Even if you don't eat honey, honeybee pollination* is incredibly important for so much of the food we eat.

3 Although RoboBees weren't developed to replace bees, roboticists, like Wood, believe that, in the future, these tiny robots might be used to pollinate a field of crops if there were a bee shortage. With two very thin wings that move rapidly – 120 times per second – RoboBees can take off and then hover in place, set down briefly, and then lift off again to move to another place, as real bees do.

4 Robotic bees won't replace real bees and we shouldn't expect them to. We still need to focus on efforts to save those vitally important creatures. But tremendous progress in the field of robotics is being made and RoboBees are one example of how technology can help us solve problems.

RoboBees and real bees compared	
RoboBee	**Honeybee**
Wings beat 120 times per second	Wings beat more than 200 times per second
Wingspan 3 cm	Wingspan 2.64 cm
Weight 80 mg	Weight (average) 120 mg

pollination *the process of spreading a powder produced by flowers to other flowers so that they can produce new seeds*

10C Using tech to take control

GRAMMAR Passives with *by* + agent

1 Complete the sentences with the correct words or phrases.

by	created by	invented	was	was created	were

1 The first colour TV to be patented in Mexico and the United States was invented _____ a Mexican engineer named Guillermo Gonzalez Camarena.

2 Some of the first photographs _____ developed by French-Brazilian inventor Hercules Florence.

3 The first artificial heart successfully used by a human _____ in 1969 by Dr Domingo Liotta, who was born in Argentina.

4 The ballpoint pen was _____ Hungarian and Argentinian journalist Laszlo Biro in the 1930s.

5 A method of changing plastic into biofuel _____ developed by Egyptian Azza Abdel Hamid Faiad.

6 A system that uses the sun's power to make water safe for drinking was _____ by Deepika Kurup.

2 Choose the correct words to complete the sentences.

1 Telescopes allow scientists to see things that can't *be seen / saw* by the human eye, such as far-off planets and stars.

2 Deserts *are thought / are thinking* by many people to be the best place to set up telescopes to look into the night sky.

3 In 1994, five men in Chile's Atacama Desert *were found / found* the highest, driest, flattest place on Earth.

4 This location in the Atacama Desert became the home of the ALMA telescope, which *is used / is using* by scientists who want answers to many questions, such as how planets are born.

5 Countries in Asia, Europe and North America *were spent / spent* $1.3 billion to establish ALMA.

6 ALMA *was planned and built / planned and built* by thousands of engineers and scientists.

3 Complete the sentences with the past simple passive voice of the verbs in brackets.

1 The report _____ (write) by the student.

2 The lift _____ (use) by people with disabilities.

3 The high mountain _____ (climb) by British explorers.

4 The designer's new necklace _____ (wear) by many people.

5 The bread _____ (make) by the new chefs.

6 The soup _____ (prepare) by Amy and Jai.

7 The animals at the zoo _____ (feed) by volunteers.

8 The room _____ (decorate) by the bride and groom's friends.

4 Read the questions. Complete the answers using the passive with *by*.

1 A Did a lot of people see the film?
  B Yes! The film _____ millions of people!

2 A Did you hear that Gonzalo lost his tablet?
  B Yes, but then it _____ his teacher.

3 A How many text messages did you get?
  B Ten. But nine _____ my mother!

4 A Who owns that restaurant?
  B It _____ Mr Ruiz.

5 A How can I pay my phone bill?
  B It can _____ cheque or by credit card.

6 A How are sweaters made?
  B They can _____ machine or by hand.

7 A Who called the police?
  B They _____ a man who saw the accident.

5 Read the sentences. Cross out the agent when it isn't necessary.

1 A great deal of the development of robots is done by the Japanese.

2 There are robots that can be controlled by a remote control.

3 Robots are programmed by people to do certain tasks.

4 Robots can take over some jobs that were done by people.

5 New uses for robots are found all the time by scientists.

6 The world's most expensive robot was sold last year by the company that made it.

7 Would you eat a meal that was prepared by a robot?

8 An alternative solution to the problem is currently being developed by someone.

6 Use the prompts to write sentences in the present or past passive voice.

1 president / elect / the people (present simple passive)

2 some / of the money / spend / the actor (past simple passive)

3 lost key / find / my brother (past simple passive)

4 problem / solve / a team of students (past simple passive)

5 emergency services / contact / a woman (past simple passive)

6 children / give / shirts to wear at the competition (present simple passive)

7 project / give / to the best candidate (present simple passive)

8 messages / send / students when school is cancelled (present simple passive)

9 exam results / announce / the local newspaper (present simple passive)

7 Change the sentences from active to passive. Include the agent when necessary.

Example: People use mobile phones to do more than make phone calls and send text messages.

Mobile phones are used to do more than make phone calls and send text messages.

1 Engineers have done work and because of this, in 2015 more than 91% of the world had better sources of water to drink.

_____

2 Energy companies use the power of the sun to bring electricity to people in sub-Saharan Africa.

_____

3 Eden Full, a student at Princeton University, developed solar panels that turn to face the sun for as long as possible each day.

_____

4 Young people in Africa use an innovative project, Text to Change, to share their thoughts about politics and advice for the future.

_____

5 People recycle food packaging to reduce waste and protect the environment.

_____

10D How to control someone else's arm with your brain

TEDTALKS

AUTHENTIC LISTENING SKILLS

1 Listen to the TED Talk extracts. Underline the words that have reduced forms. 🎧 108

1 All right, Sam, I'm going to record from your brain.
2 So I'm going to stand over here and I'm going to open up our app here.
3 Do you guys want to see some more?
4 Miguel, all right. You're going to stand right here.
5 So I'm going to find your ulnar nerve, which is probably right around here.

WATCH ▶

2 Watch the TED Talk. Are the sentences true (T) or false (F)?

1 Neuroscientists have to go to graduate school for six and a half years. _____
2 One out of five people will have a neurological disorder – a problem with their brains. _____
3 Greg Gage made an expensive piece of equipment for studying brains in special labs. _____
4 Greg asks an audience member to try his equipment to study his brain. _____
5 A person has about 80 billion neurons inside his brain. _____
6 Sam has heard what her brain sounds like before. _____

3 Choose the correct words to complete the sentences.

1 When Greg was a *high-school* / *graduate* student, he decided to make equipment for studying the brain.
2 Greg's company is called *Backyard Brains* / *DIY Equipment*.
3 Greg is going to record from Sam's *arm* / *brain*.
4 Greg asks Sam to *squeeze* / *raise* her hand.
5 Greg's equipment *can* / *cannot* be carried around.

4 Choose the correct answers.

1 What is the speaker mainly discussing?
   a how universities study brains
   b how his equipment works to study the brain
   c how people develop brain problems

2 The speaker says that he made DIY neuroscience equipment. What is *DIY*?
   a when people make their own things
   b when people make a copy of an existing design
   c when people fix a broken equipment

3 Why does the speaker mention Tim Marzullo?
   a because Tim came up with the idea by himself
   b because Tim is a graduate student
   c because Tim is his partner

4 What can be inferred about the speaker?
   a The speaker's job is to do surgery on brains.
   b The speaker went to graduate school for six and a half years.
   c The speaker didn't graduate from college.

5 Why does the speaker say: 'This is what's happening all across the world – electrophysiology! We're going to bring on the neuro-revolution.'?
   a to explain that everyone in the world is going to use only his equipment
   b to explain that there is going to be a war about neuroscience
   c to show that there is going to be a change in neuroscience

VOCABULARY IN CONTEXT

5 Choose the correct meaning of the words in bold.

1 'And one of the reasons why is that the equipment is so **complex** and so expensive that it's really only done at major universities and large institutions.'
   a not simple   **b** heavy   **c** much money

2 'I need one more **volunteer**. What is your name, sir?'
   a expert
   b chance to show something
   c a person who wants to do something

3 Greg wants to show how his equipment works. He asks for Sam to **try it out**.
   a remove it
   b attempt to use it
   c get rid of it

4 'OK, so Sam, I want you to **squeeze** your hand again.'
   a raise
   b press together strongly
   c open gently

5 Greg tells Miguel that when Sam squeezes her hand, it will feel **weird** at first.
   a strange   **b** normal   **c** painful

10E Who's in control?

SPEAKING

1 Complete the sentences about studying online with the correct phrases. Then decide if each sentence is talking about pros (P), cons (C) or both sides of an argument (B).

but on the other hand
On the one hand
One bad thing about studying online
One good thing about studying online
Studying online can be a problem
Studying online is good

(1) _____
is that you don't have to go to school to study; you can do it whenever you want or whenever you have time. _____

(2) _____
is that it's harder to get the help you need when you have a question. Sometimes you can't ask anyone and you always have to wait for a reply. _____

(3) _____
because you can do high-quality courses that cost less money and some are even free! _____

(4) _____,
you can study with people all over the world,

(5) _____,
you don't really have anyone to work with like you do in a classroom. _____

(6) _____
because the teacher can't personalize the course for your interests, so you can lose interest and give up. _____

2 Match the sentences with the responses.

1 I can't wait until we all use self-driving cars!

2 I don't think we need to go on holiday this year. We can just use virtual reality headsets and walk around the places in our own homes.

3 My brother's so popular! He's got over 3,000 friends on his social media page.

4 What do you think about artificial intelligence (AI) replacing humans in hospitals?

a OK, that's partly true, but being there yourself is good because it's the only way to experience the real life of a place.

b Really? How many of those friends does he see regularly?

c Well, on the one hand, AI can do things much more precisely, but on the other hand, AI can't understand people's needs like doctors and nurses can.

d Yes, one good thing about them is that there'll be fewer accidents.

3 Over the last decade, smartphones have become an essential part of life. As with any new technology, they bring some changes that are good and some that are bad. Make notes about the pros and cons of smartphones. Use the language you have learned for talking about pros and cons. Then listen to an example of two students discussing the question and compare this with your ideas. 🎧 109

Pros	Cons

4 Technology means that we use machines to make things that in the past we made by hand. Is it better to use machines to make things or for us to do it ourselves? Make notes on your ideas and use the language you have learned for talking about pros and cons. Then listen to an example of two students discussing the question and compare it with your ideas. 🎧 110

WRITING A formal letter of suggestion

5 Put the words in the correct order to make suggestions and support an argument.

1 some people / that / think most / While I understand / are noisy, I / people are not

_____
_____ .

2 I think / that it's / I can see / a solution / annoying, / but / we can find

_____
_____ .

3 try / rules / suggest / set / Can / that / of / I / a / we / different

_____
_____ ?

4 to / this / way / might / do / be / another / possible / It

_____
_____ .

6 Read the formal letter from a student, Ewa Nowak, to Mr Herrera, the headteacher. Then underline the information in 1–6 in the letter.

1 the reason for the letter
2 what the headteacher wants
3 the part of the rule the student agrees with
4 the name of the new set of rules suggested
5 the suggested rule about social media
6 what the new rules would allow students to do

Dear Mr Herrera,

I am writing about the new 'no laptops' rule in the library. While I understand that you want students to read the books that are in our school library, I think laptops are extremely important study tools as well. I can see that it is a problem when some students only check social media, but most of us are studying.

Can I suggest that you replace the 'no laptops' rule with a set of 'serious study' rules?
For example:
- The library is a place for study.
- Use laptops for research and study only.
- Respect others who are trying to study.
- Turn your laptop volume to mute.
- No checking social media in the library!

These rules would help to keep the library as a place for serious study, but would still allow students to use their laptops to research and write essays.

Thank you for considering this suggestion.

Yours sincerely,
Ewa Nowak

7 Read the letter from Fred Evans, a student who has a part-time job at the Cozy Café, to Ms Morris, the café owner. Complete the letter with the correct words and phrases.

but I think	can see	considering
I do not think	suggest	while
would allow	would stop	writing

Dear Ms Morris,

I am **(1)** _____ about the new 'no personal phone calls' rule for employees at the Cozy Café. My friends and I really enjoy working at the café on Saturdays, but we are worried about the new rule. I **(2)** _____ that it gives customers a bad impression, **(3)** _____ we can find a solution. **(4)** _____ I understand that employees who spend lots of time on their mobile phones at work are not doing their job properly, **(5)** _____ it is reasonable to ban *all* personal phone calls.

Can I **(6)** _____ that you replace the 'no personal phone calls' rule with a new policy?
For example:
- No more than two personal calls while at work.
- Speak quietly when taking any personal calls.
- Limit personal calls to five minutes, maximum.
- Do not take personal calls in front of customers.
- Additional personal calls for emergencies only!

These rules **(7)** _____ the annoying behaviour of some employees, but **(8)** _____ the rest of us to manage short, personal phone calls without bothering anyone.

Thank you for **(9)** _____ this suggestion.

Yours sincerely,
Fred Evans

8 Write a formal letter of suggestion about the following topic. Give reasons for your answer and support your idea with suggestions.

Games on mobile phones are a waste of time.

From now on, there is a new rule. Students are not allowed to play games on their phones during school hours.

—Mr Leeming, Headteacher

Review

1 Unscramble the letters to make words and complete the sentences.

ercasher	sveedmenoplt	rogserps
cepsors	nivnenoti	qepeminut

1 To work in a factory, you need to know how to use the _____.

2 New _____ in face-recognition technology could make it possible for us to use our face as an ID and credit card instead of carrying a wallet around.

3 Self-driving car and truck technology is making fast _____. Soon they will be driving all around us on the roads.

4 The wheel may be the most important _____ in human history.

5 Biologists do a lot of important _____ in the rainforests to discover new species of plants and animals.

6 Introducing a new medicine to the market is a long _____ that involves years of research, development, testing and waiting for government approval.

2 Match the sentences.

1 I created a new game to play on a mobile phone.

2 Last year, I didn't know anything about computers. Now I can write some simple programs.

3 The recipe was difficult to make, but I read the instructions and did it step by step.

4 I have a new flying drone. I use this small device to make it go up, come down, and turn left and right.

5 I watched a YouTube video about building a tree house. Now I want to try it!

6 I want to know more about the Cassini spacecraft.

a I followed the process.

b I can control it.

c I've made some progress.

d I'm going to do some research.

e It's my invention.

f I need some tools and equipment.

3 Find and correct the mistakes with the passive.

1 The number of people who own tablet computers predicted to reach 150 million very soon.

_____

2 Nearly fourteen hours a week on average spent using tablets, more than smartphones and PCs.

_____

3 Tablets was use by most people on weekdays, not weekends. _____

4 Nearly half of tablets are share by more than one person, but only one third of people share their smartphones. _____

5 Wifi-only tablets is preferred by most people, rather than 4G tablets. _____

6 It expects that PC usage will decrease in the next five years as tablet use increases. _____

4 Choose the correct words to complete the sentences.

1 The Bay of Bengal *was seen* / *saw* by the tourists.

2 The coach *was gave* / *gave* the instructions.

3 Rena *was spent* / *spent* the money.

4 We *are seen* / *saw* several petrol stations along the road to the airport.

5 Look at the photos. Write three or four sentences about each one using the passive.

Example: The *Titanic*

This ship was named the Titanic *because of its size. It was built in the UK and was launched into the Atlantic in 1912. It sank on its first voyage and its remains were discovered in 1985!*

The Sphinx

The Great Wall

Machu Picchu

UNIT 1

Revision

bald (adj)	/bɔːld/
beard (n)	/bɪə(r)d/
black (adj)	/blæk/
blonde (adj)	/blɒnd/
brown (adj)	/braʊn/
dark (adj)	/dɑː(r)k/
curly (adj)	/'kɜː(r)li/
glasses (n)	/'glɑːsɪz/
hair (n)	/heə(r)/
long (adj)	/lɒŋ/
short (adj)	/ʃɔː(r)t/
straight (adj)	/streɪt/
tall (adj)	/tɔːl/

Unit vocabulary

active (adj)	/'æktɪv/
calm (adj)	/kɑːm/
cheerful (adj)	/'tʃɪə(r)f(ə)l/
cool (adj)	/kuːl/
confident (adj)	/'kɒnfɪd(ə)nt/
easygoing (adj)	/ˌiːzi'gəʊɪŋ/
friendly (adj)	/'fren(d)li/
funny (adj)	/'fʌni/
happy (adj)	/'hæpi/
hard-working (adj)	/'hɑː(r)d ˌwɜː(r)kɪŋ/
helpful (adj)	/'helpf(ə)l/
honest (adj)	/'ɒnɪst/
intelligent (adj)	/ɪn'telɪdʒ(ə)nt/
kind (adj)	/kaɪnd/
lazy (adj)	/'leɪzi/
loud (adj)	/laʊd/
nasty (adj)	/'nɑːsti/
nervous (adj)	/'nɜː(r)vəs/
nice (adj)	/naɪs/
personality (n)	/ˌpɜː(r)sə'næləti/
popular (adj)	/'pɒpjʊlə(r)/
relaxed (adj)	/rɪ'lækst/
serious (adj)	/'sɪəriəs/
shy (adj)	/ʃaɪ/
smart (adj)	/smɑː(r)t/
sociable (adj)	/'səʊʃəb(ə)l/
talented (adj)	/'tæləntɪd/
weak (adj)	/wiːk/

Extension

affectionate (adj)	/ə'fekʃ(ə)nət/
annoying (adj)	/ə'nɔɪɪŋ/
careless (adj)	/'keə(r)ləs/
generous (adj)	/'dʒenərəs/
impatient (adj)	/ɪm'peɪʃ(ə)nt/
neat (adj)	/niːt/
organized (adj)	/'ɔː(r)gənaɪzd/
patient (adj)	/'peɪʃ(ə)nt/
polite (adj)	/pə'laɪt/
rude (adj)	/ruːd/
selfish (adj)	/'selfɪʃ/

Vocabulary building

be (v)	/biː/
become (v)	/bɪ'kʌm/

afraid (adj)	/ə'freɪd/
angry (adj)	/'æŋgri/
bored (adj)	/bɪː/
excited (adj)	/ɪk'saɪtɪd/
feel (v)	/fiːl/
frightened (adj)	/'fraɪt(ə)nd/
get (v)	/get/
look (v)	/lʊk/
seem (v)	/siːm/
upset (adj)	/ʌp'set/
worried (adj)	/'wʌrid/

Vocabulary in context

feel calm (phr)	/ˌfiːl 'kɑːm/
image (n)	/'ɪmɪdʒ/
language barrier (phr)	/'læŋgwɪdʒ ˌbæriə(r)/
proposal (n)	/prə'pəʊz(ə)l/
struggle (n)	/'strʌg(ə)l/

UNIT 2

Revision

apartment (n)	/ə'pɑː(r)tmənt/
bathroom (n)	/'bɑːθˌruːm/
bed (n)	/bed/
bedroom (n)	/'bedruːm/
city (n)	/'sɪti/
dining room (n)	/'daɪnɪŋ ruːm/
garden (n)	/'gɑː(r)d(ə)n/
kitchen (n)	/'kɪtʃən/
living room (n)	/'lɪvɪŋ ruːm/
quiet (adj)	/'kwaɪət/
wall (n)	/wɔːl/

Unit vocabulary

art (n)	/ɑː(r)t/
business district (n)	/'bɪznəs ˌdɪstrɪkt/
chair (n)	/tʃeə(r)/
crowded (adj)	/'kraʊdɪd/
decoration (n)	/ˌdekə'reɪʃ(ə)n/
door (n)	/dɔː(r)/
historic (adj)	/hɪ'stɒrɪk/
light (adj)	/laɪt/
modern (adj)	/'mɒdə(r)n/
refrigerator (n)	/rɪ'frɪdʒəˌreɪtə(r)/
residential area (n)	/ˌrezɪ'denʃ(ə)l 'eəriə/
rural (adj)	/'rʊərəl/
shopping district (n)	/'ʃɒpɪŋ ˌdɪstrɪkt/
sofa (n)	/'səʊfə/
stairs (n)	/steə(r)z/
suburban (adj)	/sə'bɜː(r)bən/
table (n)	/'teɪb(ə)l/
traditional (adj)	/trə'dɪʃ(ə)nəl/
urban (adj)	/'ɜː(r)bən/
walkable (adj)	/'wɔːkəb(ə)l/
window (n)	/'wɪndəʊ/

Extension

bookshelf (n)	/'bʊkˌʃelf/
cabinet (n)	/'kæbɪnət/
carpet (n)	/'kɑː(r)pɪt/
ceiling (n)	/'siːlɪŋ/

curtains (n)	/'kɜː(r)t(ə)nz/
cushion (n)	/'kʊʃ(ə)n/
drawer (n)	/'drɔːə(r)/
drive (n)	/draɪv/
floor (n)	/flɔː(r)/
lift (n)	/lɪft/
oven (n)	/'ʌv(ə)n/
sink (n)	/sɪŋk/
tap (n)	/tæp/
toilet (n)	/'tɔɪlət/

Vocabulary building

accommodation (n)	/əˌkɒmə'deɪʃ(ə)n/
communication (n)	/kəˌmjuːnɪ'keɪʃ(ə)n/
imagination (n)	/ɪˌmædʒɪ'neɪʃ(ə)n/
construction (n)	/kən'strʌkʃ(ə)n/
direction (n)	/dɪ'rekʃ(ə)n/
education (n)	/ˌedjʊ'keɪʃ(ə)n/
exploration (n)	/ˌeksplə'reɪʃ(ə)n/
location (n)	/ləʊ'keɪʃ(ə)n/

Vocabulary in context

I've got to tell you (phr)	/aɪv gɒt tə tel juː/
didn't feel right (phr)	/dɪd(ə)nt ˌfiːl 'raɪt/
elegant (adj)	/'əlɪgənt/
make perfect sense (phr)	/meɪk 'pɜː(r)fɪkt sens/
treat you well (phr)	/ˌtriːt jʊ 'wel/

UNIT 3

Revision

back (n)	/bæk/
body (n)	/'bɒdi/
dentist (n)	/'dentɪst/
doctor (n)	/'dɒktə(r)/
eyes (n)	/aɪz/
face (n)	/feɪs/
fine (adv)	/faɪn/
teeth (n)	/tiːθ/
tooth (n)	/tuːθ/

Unit vocabulary

arm (n)	/ɑː(r)m/
backache (n)	/'bækeɪk/
broken (adj)	/'brəʊkən/
chest (n)	/tʃest/
ears (n)	/ɪə(r)z/
elbow (n)	/'elbəʊ/
finger (n)	/'fɪŋgə(r)/
flu (n)	/fluː/
foot (n)	/fʊt/
head (n)	/hed/
healthy (adj)	/'helθi/
high temperature (n)	/haɪ 'temprɪtʃə(r)/
hospital (n)	/'hɒspɪt(ə)l/
ill (adj)	/ɪl/
illness (n)	/'ɪlnəs/
injury (n)	/'ɪndʒəri/
knee (n)	/niː/
leg (n)	/leg/

medicine (n)	/ˈmed(ə)s(ə)n/
mouth (n)	/maʊθ/
pain (n)	/peɪn/
patient (n)	/ˈpeɪʃ(ə)nt/
seasickness (n)	/ˈsiː,sɪknəs/
shoulder (n)	/ˈʃəʊldə(r)/
sports injuries (n)	/spɔː(r)ts ˈɪndʒəriz/
stomach (n)	/ˈstʌmək/
unwell (adj)	/ʌnˈwel/
virus (n)	/ˈvaɪrəs/

Extension

accident (n)	/ˈæksɪd(ə)nt/
ankle (n)	/ˈæŋk(ə)l/
blood (n)	/blʌd/
bone (n)	/bəʊn/
brain (n)	/breɪn/
cheek (n)	/tʃiːk/
chin (n)	/tʃɪn/
finger (n)	/ˈfɪŋgə(r)/
heart (n)	/hɑː(r)t/
lungs (n)	/lʌŋz/
neck (n)	/nek/
pump (v)	/pʌmp/
recover (v)	/rɪˈkʌvə(r)/
toe (n)	/təʊ/
wrist (n)	/rɪst/

Vocabulary building

attempt (v)	/əˈtempt/
believe (v)	/bɪˈliːv/
combine (v)	/kəmˈbaɪn/
discover (v)	/dɪˈskʌvə(r)/
entire (adj)	/ɪnˈtaɪə(r)/
find (v)	/faɪnd/
mix (v)	/mɪks/
normal (adj)	/ˈnɔː(r)m(ə)l/
sickness (n)	/ˈsɪknəs/
think (v)	/θɪŋk/
typical (adj)	/ˈtɪpɪk(ə)l/
try (v)	/traɪ/
well (adj)	/wel/
whole (adj)	/həʊl/

Vocabulary in context

institution (n)	/ˌɪnstɪˈtjuːʃ(ə)n/
hit the books (phr)	/ˌhɪt ðə ˈbʊks/
ignore (v)	/ɪgˈnɔː(r)/
pass out (phr v)	/ˌpɑːs ˈaʊt/
specialist (n)	/ˈspeʃəlɪst/
take seriously (phr)	/ˌteɪk ˈsɪəriəsli/

UNIT 4

Revision

books (n)	/bʊks/
class (n)	/klɑːs/
classroom (n)	/ˈklɑːs,ruːm/
dictionary (n)	/ˈdɪkʃən(ə)ri/
fail (v)	/feɪl/
homework (n)	/ˈhəʊm,wɜː(r)k/
lesson (n)	/ˈles(ə)n/
library (n)	/ˈlaɪbrəri/
map (n)	/mæp/
pass (v)	/pɑːs/
school bus (n)	/ˌskuːlˈbʌs/
teach (v)	/tiːtʃ/

| teacher (n) | /ˈtiːtʃə(r)/ |
| university (n) | /ˌjuːnɪˈvɜː(r)səti/ |

Unit vocabulary

attend (v)	/əˈtend/
blackboard (n)	/ˈblæk,bɔː(r)d/
class size (n)	/klɑːs saɪz/
creative (adj)	/kriˈeɪtɪv/
desk (n)	/desk/
develop (v)	/dɪˈveləp/
grade (n)	/greɪd/
notebook (n)	/ˈnəʊt,bʊk/
online learning (n)	/ˈɒnlaɪn ˌlɜː(r)nɪŋ/
primary school (n)	/ˈpraɪməri ˌskuːl/
private school (n)	/ˈpraɪvət ˌskuːl/
secondary school (n)	/ˈsekənd(ə)ri ˌskuːl/
skills (n)	/skɪlz/
state school (n)	/steɪt skuːl/
student (n)	/ˈstjuːd(ə)nt/
study (v)	/ˈstʌdi/
test (n)	/test/

Extension

after-school activities (phr)	/ˈɑːftə(r) skuːl ækˈtɪvətiz/
algebra (n)	/ˈældʒɪbrə/
ancient history (n)	/ˈeɪnʃ(ə)nt ˈhɪst(ə)ri/
bad grades (n)	/ˈbæd ˈgreɪdz/
band (n)	/ˈbænd/
biology (n)	/baɪˈɒlədʒi/
chemistry (n)	/ˈkemɪstri/
chess (n)	/tʃes/
drama club (n)	/ˈdrɑːmə klʌb/
geography (n)	/dʒiˈɒgrəfi/
geometry (n)	/dʒiˈɒmətri/
history (n)	/ˈhɪstəri/
maths (n)	/ˈmæθs/
orchestra (n)	/ˈɔː(r)kɪstrə/
physics (n)	/ˈfɪzɪks/
science (n)	/ˈsaɪəns/
social sciences (n)	/ˈsəʊʃ(ə)l ˌsaɪənsɪz/
team (n)	/tiːm/

Vocabulary building

beautiful (adj)	/ˈbjuːtəf(ə)l/
careful (adj)	/ˈkeə(r)f(ə)l/
careless (adj)	/ˈkeə(r)ləs/
skillful (adj)	/ˈskɪlf(ə)l/
thankful (adj)	/ˈθæŋkf(ə)l/
useful (adj)	/ˈjuːsf(ə)l/

Vocabulary in context

100 percent (n)	/wʌn ˈhʌndrəd pə(r)ˈsent/
go into (phr v)	/gəʊ ˈɪntuː/
in other words (phr)	/ɪn ˈʌðə(r) wɜː(r)dz/
make it to (phr)	/meɪk ɪt tuː/
producing (v)	/prəˈdjuːsɪŋ/
were in trouble (phr)	/wɜː(r) ɪn ˈtrʌb(ə)l/

UNIT 5

Review

boy (n)	/bɔɪ/
children (n)	/ˈtʃɪldrən/
cousin (n)	/ˈkʌz(ə)n/

daughter (n)	/ˈdɔːtə(r)/
divorced (adj)	/dɪˈvɔː(r)st/
family (n)	/ˈfæmli/
father (n)	/ˈfɑːðə(r)/
friends (n)	/frendz/
girl (n)	/gɜː(r)l/
husband (n)	/ˈhʌzbənd/
man (n)	/mæn/
men (n)	/men/
married (adj)	/ˈmærid/
mother (n)	/ˈmʌð(ə)r/
parents (n)	/ˈpeərənts/
single (adj)	/ˈsɪŋg(ə)l/
son (n)	/sʌn/
wife (n)	/waɪf/
woman (n)	/ˈwʊmən/
women (n)	/ˈwɪmɪn/

Unit vocabulary

aunt (n)	/ɑːnt/
best friend (n)	/ˌbest ˈfrend/
brother (n)	/ˈbrʌð(ə)r/
classmate (n)	/ˈklɑːs,meɪt/
hug (v)	/hʌg/
husband (n)	/ˈhʌzbənd/
grandfather (n)	/ˈgræn(d),fɑːðə(r)/
grandmother (n)	/ˈgræn(d),mʌðə(r)/
kiss (v)	/kɪs/
mother (n)	/ˈmʌðə(r)/
neighbour (n)	/ˈneɪbə(r)/
partner (n)	/ˈpɑː(r)tnə(r)/
say hello (phr)	/seɪ həˈləʊ/
shake hands (phr)	/ˌʃeɪk ˈhændz/
sister (n)	/ˈsɪstə(r)/
stranger (n)	/ˈstreɪndʒə(r)/
teammate (n)	/ˈtiːm,meɪt/
uncle (n)	/ˈʌŋk(ə)l/
wave (v)	/weɪv/

Extension

acquaintance (n)	/əˈkweɪntəns/
brother-in-law (n)	/ˈbrʌðə(r) ɪn lɔː/
bow (v)	/baʊ/
ex-husband (n)	/ˌeksˈhʌzbənd/
ex-wife (n)	/ˌeksˈwaɪf/
father-in-law (n)	/ˈfɑːðə(r) ɪn lɔː/
half-brother (n)	/hɑːfˈbrʌðə(r)/
half-sister (n)	/hɑːfˈsɪstə(r)/
kids (n)	/kɪdz/
mother-in-law (n)	/ˈmʌðə(r) ɪn lɔː/
nephew (n)	/ˈnefjuː/
niece (n)	/niːs/
stepbrother (n)	/ˈstep,brʌðə(r)/
stepfather (n)	/ˈstep,fɑːðə(r)/
stepmother (n)	/ˈstep,mʌðə(r)/
stepsister (n)	/ˈstep,sɪstə(r)/

Vocabulary building

cultural (adj)	/ˈkʌltʃ(ə)rəl/
emotional (adj)	/ɪˈməʊʃ(ə)nəl/
musical (adj)	/ˈmjuːzɪk(ə)l/
national (adj)	/ˈnæʃ(ə)nəl/
natural (adj)	/ˈnætʃ(ə)rəl/
traditional (adj)	/trəˈdɪʃ(ə)nəl/

Vocabulary in context

| odd (adj) | /ɒd/ |
| origins (n) | /ˈɒrɪdʒɪnz/ |

roots (n)	/ruːts/
silly (adj)	/ˈsɪli/
weird (adj)	/wɪə(r)d/

UNIT 6

Revision

afraid (adj)	/əˈfreɪd/
friendly (adj)	/ˈfrendli/
lazy (adj)	/ˈleɪzi/
nervous (adj)	/wɪə(r)d/
relaxed (adj)	/rɪˈlækst/
shy (adj)	/ʃaɪ/
worried (adj)	/ˈwʌrid/

Unit vocabulary

accept (v)	/əkˈsept/
fail (v)	/feɪl/
failure (n)	/ˈfeɪljə(r)/
imperfect (adj)	/ɪmˈpɜː(r)fɪkt/
imperfection (n)	/ˌɪmpə(r)ˈfekʃ(ə)n/
perfect (adj)	/ˈpɜː(r)fɪkt/
perfection (n)	/ˌpə(r)ˈfekʃ(ə)n/
reject (v)	/rɪˈdʒekt/
success (n)	/səkˈses/
succeed (v)	/səkˈsiːd/
successful (adj)	/səkˈsesf(ə)l/
unsuccessful (adj)	/ˌʌnsəkˈsesf(ə)l/

Extension

academic success (n)	/ˌækəˈdemɪk səkˈses/
accept responsibility (phr)	/əkˈsept rɪˌspɒnsəˈbɪləti/
condition (n)	/kənˈdɪʃən/
economic success (phr)	/ˌiːkəˈnɒmɪk səkˈses/
fail two exams (phr)	/ˈfeɪl tuː ɪɡˈzæmz/
perfect example (phr)	/ˈpɜː(r)fɪkt ɪɡˈzɑːmp(ə)l/
perfect opportunity (phr)	/ˈpɜː(r)fɪkt ˌɒpə(r)ˈtjuːnəti/
reject an idea (phr)	/rɪˈdʒekt ən aɪˈdɪə/
slightly imperfect (phr)	/ˌslaɪtli ɪmˈpɜː(r)fɪkt/
successful company (phr)	/səkˈsesf(ə)l ˈkʌmp(ə)ni/
very successful (phr)	/ˈveri səkˈsesf(ə)l/

Vocabulary building

disagree (v)	/ˌdɪsəˈɡriː/
disconnect (v)	/dɪskəˈnekt/
dishonest (adj)	/dɪsˈɒnɪst/
dislike (v)	/dɪsˈlaɪk/
immature (adj)	/ˌɪməˈtjʊə(r)/
improper (adj)	/ɪmˈprɒpə(r)/
inactive (adj)	/ɪnˈæktɪv/
incorrect (adj)	/ɪnkəˈrekt/
indirect (adj)	/ˌɪndəˈrekt/
unfinished (adj)	/ʌnˈfɪnɪʃt/
unkind (adj)	/ʌnˈkaɪnd/
unlucky (adj)	/ʌnˈlʌki/
unsuccessful (adj)	/ˌʌnsəkˈsesf(ə)l/

Vocabulary in context

courageous (adj)	/kəˈreɪdʒəs/
negotiate (v)	/nɪˈɡəʊʃieɪt/

potential (adj)	/pəˈtenʃ(ə)l/
run (v)	/rʌn/
struggle (v)	/ˈstrʌɡ(ə)l/
supportive network (phr)	/səˈpɔː(r)tɪv ˈnetˌwɜː(r)k/

UNIT 7

Revision

banana (n)	/bəˈnɑːnə/
bread (n)	/bred/
butter (n)	/ˈbʌtə(r)/
breakfast (n)	/ˈbrekfəst/
cake (n)	/keɪk/
cheese (n)	/tʃiːz/
dinner (n)	/ˈdɪnə(r)/
egg (n)	/eɡ/
fish (n)	/fɪʃ/
lunch (n)	/lʌntʃ/
milk (n)	/mɪlk/
orange juice (n)	/ˈɒrɪndʒ ˌdʒuːs/
pizza (n)	/ˈpiːtsə/
rice (n)	/raɪs/
salad (n)	/ˈsæləd/
sandwich (n)	/ˈsæn(d)wɪdʒ/
sauce (n)	/sɔːs/
soup (n)	/suːp/
sugar (n)	/ˈʃʊɡə(r)/

Unit vocabulary

apple (n)	/ˈæp(ə)l/
beef (n)	/biːf/
bitter (adj)	/ˈbɪtər/
café (n)	/ˈkæfeɪ/
chicken (n)	/ˈtʃɪkɪn/
chilli powder (n)	/ˈtʃɪli ˌpaʊdə(r)/
chocolate (n)	/ˈtʃɒklət/
choose (v)	/tʃuːz/
crisps (n)	/krɪsps/
dessert (n)	/dɪˈzɜː(r)t/
dish (n)	/dɪʃ/
drink (n)	/drɪŋk/
eat (v)	/iːt/
flavour (n)	/ˈfleɪvə(r)/
french fries (n)	/ˈfrentʃ ˌfraɪz/
fruit (n)	/fruːt/
fruit salad (n)	/ˌfruːt ˈsæləd/
hungry (adj)	/ˈhʌŋɡri/
ice cream (n)	/ˈaɪs ˌkriːm/
ingredient (n)	/ɪnˈɡriːdiənt/
lemon (n)	/ˈlemən/
meat (n)	/miːt/
order (v)	/ˈɔː(r)də(r)/
pasta (n)	/ˈpæstə/
potato (n)	/pəˈteɪtəʊ/
prawns (n)	/prɔːnz/
prepare (v)	/prɪˈpeə(r)/
salty (adj)	/ˈsɔːlti/
section (n)	/ˈsekʃən/
snack (n)	/snæk/
sour (adj)	/ˈsaʊə(r)/
spice (n)	/spaɪs/
spicy (adj)	/ˈspaɪsi/
strawberry (n)	/ˈstrɔːb(ə)ri/
sweet (adj)	/swiːt/
tomato (n)	/təˈmɑːtəʊ/
vegetable (n)	/ˈvedʒtəb(ə)l/

Extension

amount (n)	/əˈmaʊnt/
boiled (adj)	/ˈbɔɪld/
delicious (adj)	/dɪˈlɪʃəs/
fast food (n)	/ˈfɑːst ˌfuːd/
fresh (adj)	/freʃ/
fried (adj)	/ˈfraɪd/
frozen food (n)	/ˌfrəʊz(ə)n ˈfuːd/
grilled (adj)	/ɡrɪld/
home-cooked meal (n)	/ˌhəʊm kʊkt ˈmiːl/
huge (adj)	/hjuːdʒ/
taste (v)	/teɪst/
terrible (adj)	/ˈterəb(ə)l/
unhealthy (adj)	/ʌnˈhelθi/

Vocabulary building

acceptance (n)	/əkˈseptəns/
accomplishment (n)	/əˈkʌmplɪʃmənt/
development (n)	/dɪˈveləpmənt/
disappearance (n)	/ˌdɪsəˈpɪərəns/
farmer (n)	/ˈfɑː(r)mə(r)/
planners (n)	/ˈplænə(r)z/

Vocabulary in context

global (adj)	/ˈɡləʊb(ə)l/
household (n)	/ˈhaʊsˌhəʊld/
invest (v)	/ɪnˈvest/
resources (n)	/rɪˈzɔː(r)sɪz/
tackle (v)	/ˈtæk(ə)l/

UNIT 8

Revision

cheap (adj)	/tʃiːp/
customer (n)	/ˈkʌstəmə(r)/
department store (n)	/dɪˈpɑː(r)tmənt ˌstɔː(r)/
(not) for sale (phr)	/(nɒt) fɔː(r) seɪl/
expensive (adj)	/ɪkˈspensɪv/
market (n)	/ˈmɑː(r)kɪt/
price (n)	/praɪs/
save money (phr)	/ˈseɪv ˈmʌni/
shop online (phr)	/ʃɒp ˈɒnlaɪn/
shoppers (n)	/ˈʃɒpə(r)z/
shopping centre (n)	/ˈʃɒpɪŋ ˌsentə(r)/
spend money (phr)	/ˌspend ˈmʌni/

Unit vocabulary

advertise (v)	/ˈædvə(r)taɪz/
design (v)	/dɪˈzaɪn/
grow (v)	/ɡrəʊ/
manufacture (v)	/ˌmænjʊˈfæktʃə(r)/
material (n)	/məˈtɪəriəl/
option (n)	/ˈɒpʃ(ə)n/
pick (v)	/pɪk/
recycle (v)	/riːˈsaɪk(ə)l/
sell (v)	/sel/
throw away (phr v)	/θrəʊ əˈweɪ/

Extension

advertisement (n)	/ədˈvɜː(r)tɪsmənt/
afford (v)	/əˈfɔː(r)d/
antique (adj)	/ænˈtiːk/
bargain (n)	/ˈbɑː(r)ɡɪn/
delivered (adj)	/dɪˈlɪvə(r)d/
discount (n)	/ˈdɪskaʊnt/

display (n)	/dɪˈspleɪ/
second-hand (adj)	/ˌsekənd ˈhænd/
trade (v)	/treɪd/

Vocabulary building

air pollution (n)	/eə(r) pəˈluːʃ(ə)n/
billboard (n)	/ˈbɪlˌbɔː(r)d/
rainforest (n)	/ˈreɪnˌfɒrɪst/
sea life (n)	/ˈsiː ˌlaɪf/
supermarket (n)	/ˈsuːpə(r)ˌmɑː(r)kɪt/
TV show (n)	/ˌtiː ˈviː ˌʃəʊ/
video game (n)	/ˈvɪdiəʊ ɡeɪm/
website (n)	/ˈwebsaɪt/

Vocabulary in context

cause a change (phr)	/ˈkɔːz ə ˈtʃeɪndʒ/
do as you say (phr)	/ˈduː əz juː ˈseɪ/
in a way that (phr)	/ˈɪn ə ˈweɪ ˈðæt/
take action (phr)	/teɪk ˈækʃ(ə)n/
walk your talk (phr)	/wɔːk jɔː tɔːk/

UNIT 9

Revision

actor (n)	/ˈæktə(r)/
artist (n)	/ˈɑː(r)tɪst/
boss (n)	/bɒs/
businessperson (n)	/ˈbɪznəsˌpɜː(r)s(ə)n/
cook (n)	/kʊk/
driver (n)	/draɪvə(r)/
guide (n)	/ɡaɪd/
photographer (n)	/fəˈtɒɡrəfə(r)/
receptionist (n)	/rɪˈsepʃ(ə)nɪst/
teacher (n)	/ˈtiːtʃə(r)/
tour guide (n)	/ˈtʊə(r) ˌɡaɪd/
waiter / waitress (n)	/ˈweɪtə(r)/ /ˈweɪtrəs/

Unit vocabulary

accountant (n)	/əˈkaʊntənt/
architect (n)	/ˈɑː(r)kɪˌtekt/
chef (n)	/ʃef/
chief executive (n)	/ˌtʃiːf ɪɡˈzekjʊtɪv/
cleaner (n)	/ˈkliːnə(r)/
construction worker (n)	/kənˈstrʌkʃ(ə)n ˈwɜː(r)kə(r)/
dentist (n)	/ˈdentɪst/
electronic engineer (n)	/ˌelekˈtrɒnɪk ˌendʒɪˈnɪə(r)/
factory worker (n)	/ˈfæktəri ˈwɜː(r) kə(r)/
firefighter (n)	/ˈfaɪə(r)ˌfaɪtə(r)/
lawyer (n)	/ˈlɔːjə(r)/
manager (n)	/ˈmænɪdʒə(r)/
nurse (n)	/nɜː(r)s/
office worker (n)	/ˈɒfɪs ˈwɜː(r)kə(r)/
paramedic (n)	/ˌpærəˈmedɪk/
police officer (n)	/pəˈliːs ˈɒfɪsə(r)/
salesperson (n)	/ˈseɪlzˌpɜːrsən/
shop manager (n)	/ʃɒp ˈmænɪdʒə(r)/
software developer (n)	/ˈsɒf(t)ˌweə(r) dɪˈveləpə(r)/

Extension

adventure (n)	/ədˈventʃə(r)/
assistant (n)	/əˈsɪst(ə)nt/
application (n)	/ˌæplɪˈkeɪʃ(ə)n/

benefit (n)	/ˈbenəfɪt/
career (n)	/kəˈrɪə(r)/
challenge (n)	/ˈtʃæləndʒ/
CV (n)	/ˌsiː ˈviː/
employed (adj)	/ɪmˈplɔɪd/
employment (n)	/ɪmˈplɔɪmənt/
excitement (n)	/ɪkˈsaɪtmənt/
an expert (n)	/ən ˈekspɜː(r)t/
freedom (n)	/ˈfriːdəm/
full-time (adj)	/ˈfʊlˈtaɪm/
get a job (phr)	/ˌget ə ˈdʒɒb/
a hard worker (phr)	/ə hɑː(r)d ˈwɜː(r)kə(r)/
in charge (phr)	/ɪn ˈtʃɑː(r)dʒ/
internship (n)	/ˈɪntɜː(r)nˌʃɪp/
out of work (adj)	/ˈaʊt əv ˈwɜː(r)k/
professional (adj)	/prəˈfeʃ(ə)nəl/
salary (n)	/ˈsæləri/
unemployed (adj)	/ʌnɪmˈplɔɪd/

Vocabulary building

borrow from (phr v)	/ˈbɒrəʊ ˌfrɒm/
take from (phr v)	/ˈteɪk ˌfrɒm/
work on (phr v)	/ˈwɜː(r)k ˌɒn/

Vocabulary in context

curiosity (n)	/ˌkjʊəriˈɒsəti/
focus on (phr v)	/ˈfəʊkəs ɒn/
tough (adj)	/tʌf/
use up (phr v)	/ˌjuːz ˈʌp/

UNIT 10

Revision

camera (n)	/ˈkæmrə/
mobile phone (n)	/ˈməʊbaɪl ˌfəʊn/
computer (n)	/kəmˈpjuːtə(r)/
machine (n)	/məˈʃiːn/
printer (n)	/ˈprɪntər/
programme (v)	/ˈprəʊɡræm/
tablet (n)	/ˈtæblət/
texts (n)	/ˈteksts/

Unit vocabulary

control (v)	/kənˈtrəʊl/
development (n)	/dɪˈveləpmənt/
digital (adj)	/ˈdɪdʒɪt(ə)l/
equipment (n)	/ɪˈkwɪpmənt/
invention (n)	/ɪnˈvenʃ(ə)n/
micro-robot (n)	/maɪkrəʊ ˈrəʊbɒt/
process (n)	/ˈprəʊses/
progress (n)	/ˈprəʊɡres/
remote control (n)	/rɪˈməʊt kənˈtrəʊl/
robot (n)	/ˈrəʊbɒt/
technology (n)	/tekˈnɒlədʒi/
tool (n)	/tuːl/

Extension

design (v)	/dɪˈzaɪn/
discover (v)	/dɪˈskʌvə(r)/
energy (n)	/ˈenə(r)dʒi/
explore (v)	/ɪkˈsplɔː(r)/
green technology (n)	/ˌɡriːn tekˈnɒlədʒi/
install (v)	/ɪnˈstɔːl/
partner (with) (v)	/ˈpɑː(r)tnə(r) ˌ(wɪð)/
spacecraft (n)	/ˈspeɪsˌkrɑːft/

Vocabulary building

achievement (n)	/əˈtʃiːvmənt/
achiever (n)	/əˈtʃiːvə(r)/
developer (n)	/dɪˈveləpə(r)/
disappointment (n)	/ˌdɪsəˈpɔɪntmənt/
engineering (n)	/ˌendʒɪˈnɪərɪŋ/
improvement (n)	/ɪmˈpruːvmənt/
production (n)	/prəˈdʌkʃ(ə)n/

Vocabulary in context

complex (adj)	/ˈkɒmpleks/
squeeze (v)	/skwiːz/
try it out (phr)	/ˌtraɪ ɪt ˈaʊt/
volunteer (n)	/ˌvɒlənˈtɪə(r)/

Photo credits:

002 (tl) Rawpixel.com/Shutterstock.com, **002** (tr) Nataliia Budianska/Shutterstock.com, **002** (cl) Flashon Studio/Shutterstock.com, **002** (cr) Felix Mizioznikov/Shutterstock.com, **002** (bl) Look Studio/Shutterstock.com, **002** (br) alexandre zveiger/Shutterstock.com, **004** Rawpixel.com/Shutterstock.com, **007** Dudarev Mikhail/Shutterstock.com, **009** De Visu/Shutterstock.com, **013** Theo Wargo/Getty Images, **014** (tl) Africa Studio/Shutterstock.com, **014** (tr) Jeffrey M. Frank/Shutterstock.com, **014** (tcl) Africa Studio/Shutterstock.com, **014** (tcr) Petch A Ratana/Shutterstock.com, **014** (cl) Ljupco Smokovski/Shutterstock.com, **014** (cr) elena castaldi viora/Shutterstock.com, **014** (bcl) Photographee.eu/Shutterstock.com, **014** (bcr) kibri_ho/Shutterstock.com, **014** (bl) nexus 7/Shutterstock.com, **019** (l) Somphop/Shutterstock.com, **019** (r) Angela Harburn/Shutterstock.com, **020** snowturtle/Shutterstock.com, **021** Angela N Perryman/Shutterstock.com, **024** UTBP/Shutterstock.com, **026** (bcl) stihii/Shutterstock.com, **026** (bcr) Fotos593/Shutterstock.com, **026** (bl) Dragon Images/Shutterstock.com, **026** (br) Monkey Business Images/Shutterstock.com, **026** (tl) Dudarev Mikhail/Shutterstock.com, **026** (tr) Monkey Business Images/Shutterstock.com, **026** (tcl) Piotr Krzeslak/Shutterstock.com, **026** (tcr) Estrada Anton/Shutterstock.com, **026** (r) exopixel/Shutterstock.com, **026** Hero Images/Getty Images, **027** Alexander Kirch/Shutterstock.com, **028** Hero Images/Getty Images, **031** Monkey Business Images/Shutterstock.com, **036** wavebreakmedia/Shutterstock.com, **037** (cl) PongMoji/Shutterstock.com, **038** (tl) Iulian Dragomir/Shutterstock.com, **038** (cl) Pavlin Plamenov Petkov/Shutterstock.com, **038** (cr) Jannis Tobias Werner/Shutterstock.com, **038** (bl) sirtravelalot/Shutterstock.com, **038** (br) Patricia Hofmeester/Shutterstock.com, **038** (b) maroke/Shutterstock.com, **038** (tr) nulinukas/Shutterstock.com, **039** Arlo Magicman/Shutterstock.com, **040** Africa Studio/Shutterstock.com, **043** Monkey Business Images/Shutterstock.com, **047** (tl) Mr. Luck/Shutterstock.com, **047** (tr) aliaksei kruhlenia/Shutterstock.com, **047** (bl) Ivana Milic/Shutterstock.com, **047** (br) elenabsl/Shutterstock.com, **049** (br) Iakov Filimonov/Shutterstock.com, **050** (t) Golden Pixels LLC/Shutterstock.com, **050** (cl) Daniel M Ernst/Shutterstock.com, **050** (tr) CandyBox Images/Shutterstock.com, **050** (tl) leungchopan/Shutterstock.com, **050** (cr) sanjagrujic/Shutterstock.com, **050** (bl) Odua Images/Shutterstock.com, **050** (br) Jennifer Lam/Shutterstock.com, **052** (t) sirtravelalot/Shutterstock.com, **052** (tc) Dima Sidelnikov/Shutterstock.com, **052** (bc) Odua Images/Shutterstock.com, **052** (b) aslysun/Shutterstock.com, **053** (cr) Allik/Shutterstock.com, **055** pisaphotography/Shutterstock.com, **056** (bl) apple2499/Shutterstock.com, **059** (br) PORTRAIT IMAGES ASIA BY NONWARIT/Shutterstock.com, **067** photoBeard/Shutterstock.com, **068** (bl) davidgoldmanphoto/Getty Images, **068** (left) ©Frank Heuer/laif/Redux, **068** (r) Andrey_Popov/Shutterstock.com, **069** kykykis/Shutterstock.com, **071** (br) 135pixels/Shutterstock.com, **074** (tl) Africa Studio/Shutterstock.com, **074** (tr) Gamzova Olga/Shutterstock.com, **074** (cl) indigolotos/Shutterstock.com, **074** (cr) farbled/Shutterstock.com, **074** (bl) margouillat photo/Shutterstock.com, **074** (br) Kazlouski Siarhei/Shutterstock.com, **076** (bl) Denis Rozhnovsky/Shutterstock.com, **076** (tr) oneinchpunch/Shutterstock.com, **079** Alison Hancock/Shutterstock.com, **086** (tl) Wayne0216/Shutterstock.com, **086** (tr) theskaman306/Shutterstock.com, **086** (cl) Radu Bercan/Shutterstock.com, **086** (cr) Anan Kaewkhammul/Shutterstock.com, **086** (bl) Dmitry Kalinovsky/Shutterstock.com, **086** (br) studiovin/Shutterstock.com, **088** Rich Carey/Shutterstock.com, **091** View Apart/Shutterstock.com, **095** (bl) one photo/Shutterstock.com, **096** (cr) I Wei Huang/Shutterstock.com, **099** (bl) Billion Photos/Shutterstock.com, **100** Monkey Business Images/Shutterstock.com, **103** (l) J. Lekavicius/Shutterstock.com, **103** (r) ventdusud/Shutterstock.com, **103** (c) Alison Hancock/Shutterstock.com, **107** (bl) Monkey Business Images/Shutterstock.com, **111** (bl) Willyam Bradberry/Shutterstock.com, **112** (t) Lanski/Shutterstock.com, **112** (b) Studio 72/Shutterstock.com, **115** Thierry Falise/Getty Images, **116** Babak Tafreshi/Getty Images, **117** (br) Smileus/Shutterstock.com, **121** (t) Pius Lee/Shutterstock.com, **119** (bl) Catalin Petolea/Shutterstock.com, **121** (c) Hung Chung Chih/Shutterstock.com, **121** (b) Vladislav T. Jirousek/Shutterstock.com.

Text credits:

007 'This Is Your Brain on Nature', by Florence Williams, National Geographic Magazine, January 2016. Reprinted by permission. **019** 'Pictures: Floating Cities of the Future', by Tasha Eichenseher, National Geographic Magazine, August 2012. Reprinted by permission. **031** 'Health at Every Size', by Mary Schons, National Geographic Magazine, August 2011. Reprinted by permission. **079** 'He Wants to Help You and Your Children Be Farmers', by Daniel Stone, National Geographic Magazine, February 2016. Reprinted by permission. **105** 'On a Roll: Food Trucks', by David Brindley and Gerd Ludwig, National Geographic Magazine, July 2015. Reprinted by permission.